T0067993

RESILIENCE

— IN THE —

FACE OF ADVERSITY

A Portuguese Immigrant Lives the American Dream

MARIO V. CARMO

authorHOUSE®

AuthorHouse™
1663 Liberty Drive
Bloomington, IN 47403
www.authorhouse.com
Phone: 833-262-8899

Published by AuthorHouse 03/14/2022

ISBN: 978-1-6655-5398-8 (sc)
ISBN: 978-1-6655-5399-5 (hc)
ISBN: 978-1-6655-5397-1 (e)

Print information available on the last page.

Any people depicted in stock imagery provided by Getty Images are models, and such images are being used for illustrative purposes only. Certain stock imagery © Getty Images.

This book is printed on acid-free paper.

Dedicated to my daughter Patricia and my grandchildren, so that they may know the origins of their roots. May you always be grateful for the great country in which we live and has given us so much. I would also like to thank my wife, Wanda, for her encouragement in writing this book. For as long as we have known each other, she has tried to convince me that I have lived a unique life: a life that it is worth recording for the benefit of generations to come.

CONTENTS

PREFACE

The idea for this book was first planted by my attorney. She handled a sensitive legal matter for me, and in the process, we got to know a bit about each other and became friends. She suggested that my life and life experiences were unique and that I should consider writing a book. Several friends over the years, including my daughter Patricia, have likewise suggested the idea. Most recently, my wife, Wanda, has pushed the idea at every opportunity. The COVID-19 pandemic shutdown gave me the opportunity to finally sit down and put pen to paper, as they say.

I have relied strictly on memory for this project. I will be forever thankful to my second cousin Almore and his family for helping me fill in the gaps in my father's younger years. My father was a hard person to get close to. He didn't know how to show emotion because he had grown up without a father or a mother. Although I was there for him in the final years, I was unable to get him to open up to me. What I know about him, I learned from others. Sitting and writing this book, I have realized how much I am like my dad. I never got around to telling him how grateful I am that he risked so much to give me and my siblings an opportunity to grow up in this great country called the USA. I think back and imagine how scared my parents must have been—two people with practically no education risking everything they had, leaving behind everything and everyone they knew, and moving to a foreign land whose language and customs they did not understand. Although I have faced many challenges in life, as we all do, they are negligible compared to what my parents faced, especially my father.

If I had to reduce it to one sentence, I would say this book is about living the American dream.

It is about growing up without electricity, running water, or indoor plumbing. It is about being poor but not realizing that you are because everyone around you is in the same situation. It is about one of the millions of families that come to America legally every year and ask for nothing but an opportunity—an opportunity to get an education, an opportunity to work, an opportunity to serve the great country that they have adopted as their own.

In this book, I tell a story of how I went from working full-time nights while in high school, to earning a master's degree. I describe how I went from private to Lieutenant Colonel and commanding a squadron of more than four hundred marines. I went from not speaking a word of English to writing this manuscript, from delivering newspapers, to holding a Top Secret Clearance and serving as deputy director of the Operations and Intelligence Division at Naval Space Command. How I went from arriving in this country with nothing, but the clothing on my back to a solid military career and living the American dream.

CHAPTER 1

THE EARLY YEARS

I was born on October 9, 1951, in a small village in northern Portugal. The village was a mile north of the city of Chaves and three miles from Portugal's northern border with Spain. Chaves was first settled by the Romans around the time of the birth of Christ. Along with a medieval castle, the city has a couple of other primary features. One of them is a bridge built by the Romans between 74 and 104 AD. It's still in use by pedestrians today. The locals refer to it as the Roman Bridge, but the formal name is "Ponte do Trajano", or the Trajano Bridge. It crosses the River Tamega which flows south from nearby Spain. The river provided irrigation for the vast agricultural valley which surrounded Chaves. The other major feature is the "hot springs". The spring's water is known for its medicinal purposes. The sulfur smelling water comes out of the ground at 76 degrees Celsius or approximately 168 degrees Fahrenheit. After undergoing a series of filtration processes, the sulfur smell is removed and the water is cooled sufficiently for medicinal use. The locals also drink it on a regular basis especially after a large meal. Doctors prescribe these baths for a variety of ailments. I can personally attest to their medicinal qualities after being successfully treated for a chronic nasal infection. People travel from all over Portugal and the nearby province of Galicia, Spain, for treatments in the hot baths. Archeologists recently excavated evidence of the use of these hot springs by the Romans in circa 300 AD.

Most of the births at that time happened at home with the help of a midwife. My birth was no exception. Because of my large size, my mother had to spend several days at the local hospital after my arrival. At the time, all births in Portugal were recorded in chronological order in ledgers. Parents were given thirty days from the day of birth to register their children at the local civil registry. Our closest civil registry was in Chaves, which is also the county seat. Although Chaves was just a mile or so away, villagers' busy routines often kept them from going to the city for prolonged periods of time. They were too busy trying to keep food on the table, and the registry of a child for couples who had large families was not high on their high priority list. Violation of this law led to a fine, but most folks were not worried. Since the children were born at home, parents would select a birthday that fell within the thirty-day period for registration. My father's first trip to the city following my birth was on November 10. He was one day late, so in order to avoid the fine, he registered my birth as October 10, 1951. All my documentation says I was born on that day. I had nine siblings, and with the exception of the youngest, which was born in August 1962, none were registered with their actual date of birth. As I grew up, I found that this was a common practice among families in rural Portugal. In some cases they cross calendar years. If you wanted to find out your actual date of birth, you had to check the baptism certificate at the local parish. The parents were forthcoming with the local priest because, unlike the civil authorities, the church didn't apply fines.

My mother's name was Candida Vinhais. My maternal grandparents were Manuel Vinhais and Ermelinda Rosa Pereira. My father was Carlos Neves do Carmo. He was the son of Antonio do Carmo and Eliza Maria Neves, who also went by Eliza Maria Neto. After using Neto and Neves interchangeably as a middle name, as his mother did, my dad finally settled on Neves. The interchangeable middle name became an issue when my parents submitted the application to immigrate to the U.S. They eventually settled the problem by obtaining affidavits from three prominent individuals of our village. They certified that Carlos Neto and Carlos Neves do Carmo was the same person. I suspect Neto was my great-grandmother's maiden name, and my grandmother used it as a means of honoring her mother.

My mother was eighteen and my father twenty-four when they were married in 1943. They never dated and spoke only briefly before they decided to marry. According to my mother, it was love at first sight. I never could get anything out of my dad, but I suspect that he at least had had enough of life at his cousin's and was looking to get settled. My mother would sit at the window in her room facing the street, and my father would stop briefly outside to chat as he went to and from the farming fields. My mother was the youngest of four. She was a late baby and as a result was both overprotected by her older brothers and resented by her older sister. My grandmother was forty-two when my mother was born. This would be considered a high-risk pregnancy by today's standards. In 1925, it was extremely dangerous and my grandmother knew it. Subsequently, my grandmother took out her resentment on my mother. She considered her a nuisance and gave her very little attention or affection. Neither my grandparents nor any of my mother's siblings supported her marriage to my father. Although he had been raised in the same village, my father had neither property nor deep roots in the village. When your livelihood is farming, owning land is key to your social and economic standing in the community. My dad had neither land nor social standing.

My paternal grandfather was from the province of Beira Alta in the interior of Portugal, just south of Tras-os-Montes. The provinces were much alike: rural, poor, mountainous, and largely dependent on agriculture. My paternal grandmother was from a village called Assureiras de Baixo in the county of Chaves (the county and city had the same name), not far from my parents' village, Faioes.

My maternal grandfather was born in 1878, and my maternal grandmother five years later. As far as I can determine, they were born, lived and died in the same village. My paternal grandparents were a few years younger. According to my dad, he was four years old when his father passed. We know firsthand from my paternal grandmother that my grandfather passed when he was thirty-four. Since my dad was born in 1919, some quick math puts my grandfather's birth in 1881. My grandmother was several years younger. She passed away in 1975 in her late eighties.

Our family has no explanation for how two people who lived hundreds of miles apart met and married in the late nineteenth century. The only immigration permitted by the government at the time, was to either Brazil or to the then Portuguese colonies in Africa. They, like many of their generation, opted to go to Brazil circa 1915 in search of a better life. I learned from my dad, that my grandparents had settled in the state of Sao Paulo, Brazil, near the capital city of the same name. My dad was born in Brazil in 1919, near the city of Sao Paulo. Although when asked, he would often say that he was born in Rio de Janeiro. I actually thought that he was born in Rio de Janeiro well into my adult years. I found out about Sao Paulo from my grandmother during a visit to Portugal in 1972. My dad knew he was born in Brazil; it's possible he just assumed it was in Rio de Janeiro. Although my dad was born in Brazil, the family returned to Portugal when he was four years old. Growing up, my siblings and I were told that my grandfather had passed away unexpectedly at a very young age in Brazil, and my grandmother had to return to Portugal with my dad and his younger sister, Lucia. Without any means of support, my grandmother took a job as a governess and maid for a medical doctor in Lisbon. She took my aunt Lucia with her to Lisbon, which was socially acceptable for a widow. My dad was left to be raised by a married older cousin in the village of Faioes, but, based on some firsthand information; I have since developed a different and much more plausible account. We know for certain that Aunt Lucia was born in Portugal, not Brazil. According to one of my dad's cousins, Almore, my grandparents lived briefly in my grandmother's village of Assureiras de Baixo after they returned from Brazil. Almore and my dad became good childhood friends during this time. He told me that my grandfather passed away shortly after my aunt's birth. Apparently, my grandfather had returned from Brazil gravely ill. A man does not just pass away at the age of thirty-four without a reason even in the 1920s. I suspect either a massive heart attack which is unlikely at thirty four, or tuberculosis as the cause of his death. Based on the information I have gathered, tuberculosis seems to be the more likely explanation. This disease was very common in both Portugal and Brazil in the early twentieth century. It also explains the sudden return to Portugal, a trip not made lightly in those days. Luckily, my grandmother was not afflicted. My dad was very reluctant to speak about this time of his childhood. It's possible that he was just too young to remember or that he was trying to repress the unpleasant memories of his upbringing by his cousin. I found Almore, whom I got to know quite well after my return to Portugal, to be much more forthcoming with this information. It is possible that Almore had a clearer memory of events because he was a few years older than my dad, and he wasn't as emotionally vested.

Starting when I was very little, my dad would on occasion, bring me along on his scheduled bread deliveries. Seeing me along in some cases for the first time, people would comment "what a cute little boy, is he your son?" My dad would always answer the same way, "you will have to ask his mother". As a child, I remember thinking, of course, I'm his son. Why doesn't he know that? I didn't get the joke until I was an adolescent. It was during one of these trips with my dad, that I first met his cousin Almore. I had often heard my dad tell stories of them growing up. It was at an outdoor market called a *feira* in Portugal. This one in particular was held on the grounds of a twelfth century castle (Castelo de Monforte) on the eighteenth and twenty-eighth of every month. It specialized in the sale of sheep, cattle and oxen. These animals were the staple of the local agricultural the time. My dad provided bread rolls for the eating establishments, called *tascas* in Portuguese that were set up for the occasion. The open market was approximately halfway between Faioes and Almore's village of Avelelas, so they would often meet there and had lunch. My dad later started delivering bread to two taverns in Almore's village, and as time went by and I took over the bread-delivering business, I got to know Almore and his family quiet well. Our cordial relationship resumed after I retired and returned to Portugal. It was during this time that I gathered most of the information I have about my dad's childhood. Most of our discussions took place around the fireplace on special occasions such as Christmas Eve, or Easter. My dad was always present but seldom participated in our discussion. It was then, that I was able to query Almore and obtain information I couldn't get from my dad. Perhaps it was the port wine that put us all a bit more at ease. My dad would listen but would never interrupt or interject anything into Almore's version of events. You could sense the bond between the two.

My dad's life reminds me a little of a Charles Dickens novel. The married cousin who raised him had ten children. All but one of the ten was born after the family took my father in. My dad was treated as a hired hand without salary. He never went to school or learned to read or write; however, he did learn to write his name on his own. He worked sunrise to sunset and beyond, essentially for room and board, although he never had a room. He slept in the barn with the oxen. The justification was that since he had to get up at four AM to feed and get the animals ready for an early day of work, it was more practical for him to sleep in the barn. At the dinner table, it was customary for everyone to eat from a large common tray in the middle of the table. His cousin would often wait for everyone to sit down before asking my dad to go to the wine cellar for wine. Although my dad learned to anticipate this and have the pitcher already filled, by the time he returned to the table, the large tray was often empty or nearly so. My father's aunt, his Cousin Mario's mother, lived with them and observed this practice. After a while, she took it upon herself to make a small bowl of food and put it aside before the tray went to the table. She would later give it to my dad when others weren't observing.

My dad lived with his cousin, as basically an indentured servant, until age twenty-four, when he married my mother. He had worked for his cousin and helped him raise his family for eighteen years, and he was leaving with nothing but the clothing on his back. That is not literally true, my mother said he had two pairs of underwear and three pairs of woolen socks, made out of sheep wool called *carpins* in Portuguese, two of which had holes that she had to mend. Under the circumstances, it was not surprising that my maternal grandparents were against the union. My grandparents had some means, which they came about by living frugally even by the day's standards. My mother would eventually inherit a share of the modest estate, but my father was not bringing any financial means to the marriage. My grandmother, who pretty much ran things, was not going to make things easy for the newly married couple. My grandparents gave them absolutely nothing. As my parents told it, their first meal was a pot of soup, which my dad had to teach my mom how to make. My mother got married without knowing how to cook or do any of the many other things young women were expected to know before marriage at that time. My grandmother's lack of interest in her younger daughter was evident in this lack of marriage preparation.

Like everyone else, my parents needed a marriage license to get married. There was only one problem: my grandparents had not bothered to register my dad in the Portuguese civil registry when they returned from Brazil. My dad had never attended school, so there was no record of him anywhere. Not only that, but it was 1943, and World War II was in full swing. Portugal was officially neutral but still required all male citizens to register for the draft at age twenty. Normally, the names of the individuals required to report for the military service were listed on a poster in the village square. The year my dad turned twenty, his name didn't appeared on the list of draftees, so he didn't bothered to report for his physical. He was now twenty-four years old, four well beyond the time he was required to report. At that time, it was customary for Portuguese men to complete military service before they married and settled down. My dad was

7

kind of an odd duck. He was older than the other recruits, was married, and couldn't read or write—although he was probably not alone in the last department. After three months of recruit training, the army sent him home. They said, "We will call you if we need you." They never did!

When I was around five, my dad suffered an injury that would affect him for the rest of his life. While digging up potatoes with a hoe, which was common practice at the time, he struck a rock. Pieces of the rock flew up, and one became embedded in his left eye. He didn't see a doctor right away. I'm sure they applied olive oil which was the universal cure. The nearest ophthalmologist was at the district capital in Vila Real, some forty miles away. Lack of adequate transportation, financial means, and time, along with stubbornness, led to his delay in obtaining essential treatment in a timely manner. By the time he sought help, he had lost most of the sight in his left eye. The damage was irreversible. He never complained, but the limitation was obvious. My first visit to Vila Real was with my dad to see his ophthalmologist. I recall the trip well, we went by bus. Unfortunately, there was nothing further the doctor could do.

My earliest recollections come from when I was five to six years of age. I was the fourth child to come along. The first two had not survived measles and chicken pox, childhood diseases common at the time. The first, Adelia, named after my mother's older sister, had lived until age three. They lost the second child at age two. My sister Linda (Ermelinda), named after my maternal grandmother, was born in March 1949. When she was seven, she left home to live and attend school in a convent in Sao Joao da Madeira, a couple of hundred miles away. We saw her only during summer vacation. My parents had used my mother's aunt who had risen to the position of Mother

Superior in the convent to get my sister in. They had to pay a small monthly stipend, but it was worth it. It was also one less mouth to feed at home and one less person to worry about as we figured out our sleeping arrangements. We were already sleeping three to a bed. Two lay one way, and the third slept with his head at the foot of the bed.

We lived in a rented single room. A donkey and a pig were sheltered in the ground stable below us. We used the donkey to transport bread to customers from the small bakery my parents operated. The bread from our village had a great reputation in the region. There were a lot of families in the business, so my parents had decided to take a shot at it as well. After some on the job training, my mother would do the baking, and my father would deliver the bread. Before long, my mother had to hire someone to help her. I will discuss this operation and my role in it later. It was customary to slaughter pigs in December or January. The exact time was determined by the weather. The cold weather was essential, otherwise the meat would spoil. We did not have electricity and therefore, had no refrigeration. We also lacked running water and indoor plumbing. However, we did have a small hole in a corner of the house behind the door. There, we could perform our necessities at night without going outside and joining the animals in the stable. There was always plenty of fresh straw to spread every morning.

I did not consider myself poor. We had a small bakery business, so we always had bread and the business generated cash. My dad also leased some farmland for crops, so we always had plenty of potatoes and seasonal fresh vegetables. Everyone in our village as well as surrounding villages lived much the same way. That was life in rural northern Portugal in the late 1950s and early 60s. Agriculture was all there was. If you had a good year, the prices were low, and you made very little profit. In a bad year, you barely made ends meet. Life was hard! My dad had a system. Around springtime, he would sell the cured pig hams. They would normally bring in enough money to cover the seed and fertilizer for the spring seeding/planting. The remainder of the pig would be a big part of the family's sustenance for the remaining of the year. All the byproducts were carefully harvested and smoked. Everything in a pig was edible, from the snout to the feet and tail.

I started elementary school at age seven, as was required by Portuguese law. The school year went from October to early June. There was no spring vacation. The only time off was the week between Christmas and New Year's. Compulsory education went to fourth grade. In the middle of the twentieth century, Portugal continued to be primarily an agricultural society. The school year was planned around the harvest season, which started in June and ended with the grape/wine harvest in late September or early October. Boys and girls as young as six or seven were expected to help in this endeavor.

My Catholic education, or catechism, was held every Sunday afternoon. It actually started when children were six years old, one full year before school. I am not quite sure why because we didn't learn to read until we started school, but we heard a lot of bible stories. We learned prayers through continuous repetition. Portugal, being a Catholic nation, everyone's Catholic education was expected to cover first communion and confirmation at a minimum. First communion was easy because the local parish priest conducted the ceremony every spring. Confirmation required the bishop of the local diocese. This was normally the only time we saw the bishop. He would make the trip to our parish every three to four years. The bishop for our parish, which consisted of three different villages in my case, visited us in May 1959. The timing was perfect for me. By the time I was eight, my formal religious education was completed.

I thought this would leave me Sunday afternoons free to play soccer with my friends rather than go to religious education. However, my parents had something else in mind. I was now required to take my uncle's oxen out to pasture every Sunday afternoon. This wasn't exactly a surprise, because I had performed that same task twice a day for years before I started elementary school at age seven. In the morning, I would take them to graze up to the mountains. In the afternoon, I would drive them to the valley. I often got in trouble with my aunt for bringing the oxen home too early in the mornings—too early being before noon. In the afternoon, I could guide myself by the sunset and have them home by then. In the morning, there were few folks around the mountain paths from whom I could get the time. I didn't have a watch, and as a child, I didn't really have a good concept of time. During one of those dressing-downs that my aunt would often give me for bringing the oxen in too early, my mother happened to drop in. She was outraged by the way I was being treated, so the arrangement stopped. I then had Sunday afternoons free to play soccer with friends again. I finished fourth grade in July 1962. I like to think I was a pretty good student. At least I had good grades, despite missing school one day per week on average. Teachers accepted this because large families needed the older children to help with chores. I was ten years old and ready to go out and earn a living. Elementary school in Portugal consisted of reading, writing, history, and the four functions of arithmetic (adding, subtracting, multiplication, and division). Oh yes, there was also geography, lots of geography. Not only was the map of Portugal covered extensively, but we also studied all the colonized Portuguese territories throughout the world. The great discoveries of Portugal in the fifteenth century were covered thoroughly. The Portugal of my childhood might have been a poor and politically insignificant country run by a ruthless dictator, but the regime wanted every citizen to know that Portugal had once been one of the greatest powers in the world. It is also one of Europe's oldest independent nations, going back to 1142.

In Portugal at the time, education was very expensive. Local villages had elementary schools, but high schools were found only in the larger cities. This required either transportation, which was not available, or finding a home or other place where parents were required to pay room and board. Another option was one of the many seminaries run by the Catholic Church. The studies, along with room and board, were free, but life was hard for adolescent boys, and few made it to the priesthood. The good news was that high school credits were transferable, and many students took advantage of this. Not everyone has the vocation for the priesthood. Asking a child to make that decision at the age of eleven or twelve is unreasonable.

My best friend was going to the seminary in Fatima, and I wanted to join him very badly. My parents, however, would have none of it. My older sister was already away at the convent, so I had to stay put and help raise my siblings. In Portugal, it was customary for families to choose one child to get a formal education. Sometimes it was the oldest, but most often, it was the youngest, after the family was a little better established. All the other siblings would work toward that goal. In our house, I realized that my sister was the one who had been chosen. I still remember a conversation with my mother. She was the disciplinarian. My dad would raise his voice on occasion, but my mother was the one we had to fear. She sat me down and said, "You are the oldest boy—you are going to have to help raise your brothers and sisters." That was the end of any discussion about me going off to the seminary. Incidentally, my best friend, Albano, remained at the seminary until he finished high school. Like the vast majority, he just didn't feel the calling. After completing military service, he obtained a bachelor's degree in statistics and was later employed by the Portuguese government in the National Statistics Department, where he worked until retirement.

In retrospect, I shouldn't have been surprised by my parents' decision. Education wasn't important to them. I would run into this same dilemma years later in the US, but with a different outcome. My dad had never stepped inside a classroom, and my mother had gone only as far as third grade. The teacher had contacted my grandmother at the end of my mother's third-grade and told her there was no reason for my mother to return the following year, she knew the essentials for a girl. In addition to my sister Linda, who was away, there were four of us children at home at that time, all two years apart in age: my sister Miquelina, whom we all called Micky, my brothers Carlos, Antonio, and me. Antonio, whom we called Toze, was born on Christmas Eve 1957. My mother told us he was a gift from the baby Jesus. I remember thinking, why couldn't he just bring us cookies and candy like every other year. In 1960 my mother had a baby girl, who passed away a few days after birth. She didn't live long enough to be baptized and I don't recall my parents having given her a name. Two years later, just like clockwork, my brother Rui was born. That made six. Add my parents, and that was a lot of mouths to feed. After my brother Toze was born, we could not fit four into a single bed. My sister Micky and I started sleeping with my maternal grandparents. After dinner, my mother would walk us up the street to my grandparents' home. I slept with my grandfather, Micky with my grandmother. Initially, my mother would return to pick us up every morning, but before long we were able to make the way back by ourselves.

Managing both the farm and the small bakery business wasn't easy for my dad. Now that I had finished my compulsory education, I could become a big help to him. He could focus on farming while I took over delivering the bread from our small bakery. When I was younger, he had used me to deliver bread on the days when he had to irrigate the crops or when he had enjoyed a little more wine than normal the night before. My dad had a very low tolerance for alcohol, so it didn't take much to make him unable to function the following day. This didn't happen often, but when it did, my mother really let him have it. I could tell it was hard on my mother to send me out, especially on bad weather days. As time went by and I got older, it became a little easier, but I was still a child.

I still remember the first time I went out alone. It was during the wheat harvest and some of the customers had made larger purchases because they had hired hands to feed. Consequently, my dad ran out of bread. When he got home, my mother had a fresh batch waiting which she had made for the following day. However, my dad couldn't return to the route because the crops needed irrigation. I heard the conversation between my dad and my mother. Either my mother or I would have to go, but she had my younger brothers and sister to look after and now additional bread to bake for the following day. Neither appeared to be pleased with the choice, but it had to be me. I was no more than six or so. I had no idea how to get to where I was going. My dad's advice: "**Just let the donkey go where he wants to go. He makes this trip every day.**" He was right; the donkey (my dad called him "Russo," which means blond, although he had a salt and pepper coat), did know the way. He got me there and back. That hot afternoon in the month of July was the first of many trips before I started elementary school.

By the time I was eight years old, my father relied on me regularly to make the primary morning run. The run was about nineteen kilometers, nearly twelve miles. I left home at 5:00 a.m. and returned at approximately four in the afternoon. It seemed to me like the cemetery of every village was along my route. During the winter months, I would often go by these cemeteries while it was still dark. I would purposely look away as I walked past the cemeteries. I was scared to look in their direction because of all the silly ghost stories we all hear as children. Once I finished school, I made this trip six days per week. The task required walking either behind or in front of the donkey on the way out. I couldn't very well sit on the bread, and then I rode the donkey home.

When I first started making deliveries, customers would literally stick the money in my shoe, so I would not lose it. On more than one occasion, the donkey stumbled, and the sacks of bread fell off. I would stand by the donkey in the road, waiting for someone to come by and help me reload the sacks. At first, I would stand there crying, but after a few episodes, I realized that eventually someone would come by and help.

The passing of my maternal grandparents in 1960 had a significant impact on our lives. The passing of my grandmother on August 14, 1960, coincided with a visit from my paternal grandmother, who traveled by train from Lisbon. My dad and I took the donkey and went to meet her at the train station in Chaves. It was the first time I had seen her. She would be staying with my dad's cousin Mario during this visit, the same cousin who had raised my dad. She seemed to have more affection for him than for her own son. My dad was hurt, but she knew we didn't really have a place for her to sleep. My father's relationship with his older cousin had always been strained. My dad never forgave his cousin for the way he had treated him. However, there was one incident in particular that he cited. It was a full year after my dad had left his house, married my mother and had completed his military obligation, which was an important symbolic step by local costumes. As my dad told the story, he was standing around at the local tavern on a Sunday afternoon, talking to friends. My dad lit up a cigarette, and his cousin, who happened to be nearby, took that as an act of disrespect. In those days, sons did not smoke in front of their parents, as a sign of respect. His cousin took his hand and crushed the cigarette on my dad's face. A fracas broke out between the two. They never spoke again, but my dad continued to have a cordial relationship with all of his cousin's sons. They remembered my dad as someone who had helped raise them.

When we got home from meeting my paternal grandmother at the station, we learned that my grandmother Ermelinda had passed. It was not a total surprise; both she and my grandfather had been bedridden for months. My grandfather Manuel passed away three months later, in November 1960. She was seventy-seven, and he was eighty-two. Both had looked much older, maybe because I saw them through a child's prism or maybe because they had worked themselves to death, like many of their generation. They had grown up during difficult times and lived through the Great Depression. The depression in Portugal coincided with the Spanish Civil War. The Spanish border is five miles away, so their daily lives were impacted considerably by the war. Despite these difficulties, in their frugal ways they had managed to leave behind a reasonably sizable estate. Most persons of their generation measured success in the amount of land they owned. My maternal grandparents did not leave much money, but they did leave several buildings in the village and a fair amount of land to be divided among their three offspring. The sale of one of those properties, a vineyard inherited by my parents, would later generate sufficient funds to cover the expenses of our family's immigration to the United States. Originally there had been two brothers and two sisters in my mother's family, but my uncle Mario, after whom I was named, died at the age of twenty-three. He tragically passed away six months after he was married. From all indications, he passed because of an adverse reaction to an injection possibly penicillin.

After my grandparents passed, life got considerably better. We could finally afford to move out of the one-room rented house. My dad bought a house adjacent to a building we had inherited from my grandparents and converted the two buildings into one residence. We now had a place with three bedrooms, although one was a converted loft over the wine cellar.

From the time I finished school in July 1962, until we immigrated in February 1964, my dad pretty much dedicated himself to farming, while I handled the bread-delivery side of the business. I made different versions of essentially the same trip six and sometimes seven days per week. I had a set routine. I left the house by 5:00 a.m., and my mother would get up every morning to help me load and see me off. I think she also did it to control the business. She wanted to ensure the number of rolls I packed coincided with the amount of money I brought home. She was smart enough not to leave the business in the hands of an eleven year old child. A child with money can develop a lot of bad habits. It never happened in my case, but the potential was there. She would test me from time to time, throwing in a few extra rolls on occasion and shorting me at other times to see my reaction.

On my eleventh birthday, in October 1962, I got a big surprise. My mother got up early, as usual, to help me count the rolls and see me off. All of a sudden, she pulled a box out from under her apron. It was my first watch. I can still remember the brand; it was a *Flavia*. She made a point of telling me it had cost three hundred escudos, which was the Portuguese currency. (As a member of the European Union, Portugal would elect to adopt the euro in 2002, along with eighteen other countries.) Accounting for inflation, this would be about thirty dollars today. I was ecstatic. I took the gift as a sign that I was now making a full contribution to the household.

A few months prior to my birthday, there was another development that changed our lives. Electricity was introduced to our and two adjacent villages, which made up the parish. My parents now had the means to wire the house for electricity, and they did. We kids were very excited. No more walking around with fuel lanterns after dark. The streets lights were lit until midnight. We could move around the village after dark without bumping into walls or walking into puddles. We even had light bulbs in the barns where we kept the animals—now that was progress. A few of the families that were better-off bought refrigerators. There was talk that one or two families were thinking about buying a TV. The whole village talked about nothing else.

A man came by the house, trying to sell my parents a small table radio. My father was reluctant. The price seemed high, one thousand escudos. The salesman, hoping to convince my father, offered to leave it until his next trip to the village. One Sunday afternoon, my oldest sister Linda (who was home for summer vacation) and I had a disagreement on what to listen to. She wanted to listen to music. I wanted to listen to sports. She pulled one way; I pulled another. Before we knew it, the radio fell to the floor. The radio stopped playing. She and I said nothing. When the salesman came by to check on the radio, my dad told him the darn thing didn't work, so he didn't want it. Well, we didn't get a radio, but we didn't get into trouble either. My sister and I kept that secret until long after we were both adults.

CHAPTER 2

THE TRANSITION

Sometime in late 1962 or early 1963, my parents became aware of a new law passed by the United States Congress that allowed individuals born in South America to immigrate to the United States. This news coincided with rumors that the Portuguese government was looking to implement new health and safety regulations on bakeries, which would put small businesses like my parents out of business. Our village was known for the quality of our bread. Forty to fifty percent of families in the village were involved in some aspect of the business. The idea being floated was that some sort of a co-op be established. My parents were reluctant to join. It would require an upfront investment, but no one had answers to many of the questions being asked.

My parents took a trip to the US consulate in the city of Porto in northern Portugal, to obtain firsthand information on this new immigration program. They returned cautiously optimistic about our chances to immigrate to the United States. The first thing they had to do was obtain proof that my dad had been born in Brazil. He didn't have a birth certificate. My dad had to find someone in Brazil who would go to the city where he was born and obtain a copy of his birth certificate. However, he didn't know the name of the city where he had been registered, just the general area. It was decided that the best place to start was the local churches. They were lucky;

they found my father's baptism record in one of the first few churches they searched. Once they had the church, they checked the closest civil registry and found my dad's name. With a copy of my father's birth certificate in hand, my parents were ready to proceed with the immigration application.

It took approximately eighteen months to gather all the records required and to wait our turn in the queue. The last two steps were key to this process. My parents had to find someone in the United States who would be responsible for our financial support during our first two years. The document was called an affidavit of support. We contacted my godmother's father, who had immigrated many years earlier and was now a letter carrier in Westchester County, New York. He quickly agreed to sponsor us. Next was the physical examination at the US consulate in Porto. We were all healthy, but worried about what impact if any the reduced vision in my dad's left eye could have on the final decision. My parents were forthcoming with the information to the medical officer, and it turned out not to be a problem.

The next step was to sell some of our assets, so we could finance our travel expenses. My parents also needed additional money to cover several months of family expenses once we arrived. The last step was to pick up our visas at the US consulate in Porto. The visas were the key to our being authorized entry into the United States. We said our goodbyes to our friends and family and headed for Porto by train. From Porto we would take the train to Lisbon and then a flight to New York City. However, when so many contingencies are based on one another, something is always subject to go wrong. Murphy's Law was alive and well. When we got to the US consulate to pick up our visas, we encountered an unexpected problem. It turned out that the family friend who had sent us the affidavit of support had recently retired from his job as a letter carrier. Based on State Department requirements, his new retirement pay no longer qualified him to sponsor a family of eight. This was devastating news to my parents.

We kids were aware that there was a glitch with the paper work. We would not be leaving for *Lisbon on the date scheduled. Meanwhile, my parents were trying to keep a cool* head and come up with an alternative, and that is exactly what they did. However, there would be a delay of at least two weeks. Having said our goodbyes to relatives and friends in our village, my parents didn't want to return home and have to explain the reason for our delay. I'm sure there was the factor of pride in their decision.

We were staying at *"Pensao"*; it's similar to what we know as a bed and breakfast. My parents had selected the place largely because of its affordability. With hindsight, it had been a wise decision, because the next two weeks would be eating into the cash they were bringing as a cushion to their start in the United States. Working diligently through telephone calls and telegrams, my parents were able to find another sponsor in Connecticut. His name was Joao Pereira. My father knew him casually. He had lived in the village adjacent to ours. He had been in the U.S for five or six years and presumably in a position to be able to help us. He readily agreed. The new document arrived in less than two weeks. My parents returned to the U.S. Consulate for the much sought after Visas and we were on our way. Our whole family remains grateful to our sponsor to this day. In addition to picking us up at JFK Airport in New York, in twenty-degree weather in the middle of a snowstorm, he was also able to find an apartment for us to move into. It was tight, but it was an upgrade from our previous living arrangements. In those days, it was common for immigrant families to go out of their way to help newcomers.

Our sponsors also found jobs for both of my parents, who promptly went to work the day after they arrived. My mother went to work in a pocketbook factory making minimum wage, which was $1.25 per hour. She was paid in cash, and she brought home just under forty dollars for forty hours of work. My dad went to work setting forms for house foundations. He made $2.50 per hour. One of the daughters of our sponsor took care of getting my siblings and

I enrolled in school. The youngest, Rui, was only eighteen months old. They found a babysitter for him as well. We couldn't have asked for a better sponsor.

Two weeks after our arrival, I had an after school paper route with thirty-two customers. I made two cents per newspaper on Monday through Saturday and a nickel on the Sunday paper, which made my profit seventeen cents per week per customer. I provided my meager earnings to my mother to help with household expenses. We had two people working full-time and eight mouths to feed. However, someone was taking two newspapers from my stack every day. In order to have enough newspapers, I had to order and pay for thirty-four. I tried to call the newspaper office to make them aware of my dilemma, but I couldn't make myself understood over the phone. The first English words I learned were "newspaper boy, collect?" I collected sixty-seven cents from each customer every Friday. My best customer was a bar. The bartender gave me two bags of Planters peanuts and seventy-five cents every Friday.

Approximately one year after we arrived in the US, my sister Linda turned sixteen years old. She was attending high school at the time. My parents did not give her much of a choice about her next step; she quit school and went to work full-time with our mom. She may have lived a privilege life compared to the rest of us in Portugal, but here she was going to pull her own weigh. Right around this time, I decided that although I could do the newspaper route after school, it wasn't very profitable. A national rental-car franchise was run by two brothers-in-law for whom I delivered newspapers. They also ran a car wash. I figured the car wash was my best shot for a new job. I knew they were busy on Saturdays. I asked my dad to accompany me, but I did all the talking. I asked Nick, one of the owners, if he had any openings. He said, "Sure, grab a towel." The pay was minimum wage, $1.25 per hour, a lot better than my pay for my paper route. I worked nine hours on Saturdays (no lunch break) and five on Sundays. My new job brought in fourteen dollars per week after taxes.

After a while, I started to stop by after school during the week, and on occasion, Nick would put me to work. He assumed I was sixteen when he hired me, but he never asked me the question directly. I never corrected his assumption. Later he asked me to bring in my working papers. At the time, they were required for anyone under eighteen years of age to work. I somehow just kept forgetting them. That summer, I worked full-time. On payday, I would keep a few dollars for pocket change and give the rest to my mother. She ran the house finances. My brother Carlos got an after-school and weekend job at a neighborhood Italian market. In addition to groceries, the owner also had a butcher shop. He stocked shelves and made deliveries. After a few years, my mother opened savings accounts and deposited part of what we gave her in our accounts.

We lived in the two-bedroom apartment for two years. I recall that my parents paid fifty dollars per month in rent. The only heat in the apartment during the winter months was provided by a heating oven in the kitchen. Too bad no one slept in the kitchen. My siblings and I were growing up. A two-bedroom apartment for eight of us was no longer practical. My parents found a three-bedroom apartment a few blocks away in the middle of the Portuguese community. They paid eighty dollars per month, but by now they could afford it. My sister Linda was working full-time, and I was making a little more at the car wash. Two years after that, we moved again, this time to a two-family house just two blocks away. My parents had saved enough for a down payment on the small house. They continued to rent the upstairs to a longtime tenant while we occupied the downstairs. My parents had their own room, the girls had a room, and the boys had a room. We still had just one bathroom for the eight of us, but we made do. Life was improving gradually.

Once I turned sixteen and was attending high school, I had another one of those important conversations with my mother. One might think this would be a father–son conversation, but in our household, my mother took the lead. She made it clear: now that I was sixteen, I had to increase my contribution to the household. She came right out and said, "If you want to stay in school, you have to find a full-time night job". Sons of other families she knew were doing it, so I should be able to do it also. She was right. I knew a couple of Portuguese friends in high school who were in the same situation. One of them luckily had a car. Working through them, I was able to get a job at the same factory, making scissors. High school went from 8:30 a.m. to 2:17 p.m., and my work shift was from 3:30 p.m. to midnight. I would run home after school, change, and grab a bite to eat before my friend came by with the car picked me up around 3:10 p.m. There were now three of us working the same shift, all Portuguese from the same neighborhood. The two riders gave the driver five dollars every Friday for gas money. On Friday nights, the three of us would go out after work and share a pizza. On one of those rainy Friday nights, I heard for the first time that Dr. Martin Luther King Jr. had been shot. Up to that point in my life, I had never heard of Martin Luther King Jr. There was so much fuss being made about this on the radio that I remember asking who this guy was. Civil rights weren't high on my radar at that time in my life. The following Monday morning, very little got done in school. The African American students stayed out of class and protested for several days. It was a powder keg, but with time things cooled off. In retrospect, the administrators did an outstanding job, keeping things from getting out of control.

Two months later, I was on my way to school and heard Robert F. Kennedy had been shot. Apparently, some nut had shot and killed him at a rally after the California presidential primary. I picked up my girlfriend, skipped school, and went to a local park. We were so shocked that we listened to the radio news all day. On any other day, we would have been listening to music. All of this was going on in the midst of the Vietnam War. I remember thinking that the world was changing.

With the hours I was keeping, I didn't have a lot of time to study. The goal was to do enough school work to get by. From time to time,

I would get an opportunity to work overtime, but that was practically impossible to do with one car amongst the three of us. On several occasions, I decided to take the overtime and walk home. It was a twenty- to thirty-minute walk at 2:00 a.m. At this point, my parents decided that it was time for me to get my own car. I already had a driver's license. My parents bought me a 1967 Camaro for $2,700. They gave me a loan of $1,000 (later forgiven), and I had an $88 monthly payment plus car insurance. A first car is a big step in any teenager's life, and I was no exception. I was no longer dependent on my friend for transportation to work. I soon found another job with better pay at another factory. This job also allowed me to work based on piecework. Technically, I could perform ten hours of work in eight hours. Between school and the full-time job, I was getting by on five to six hours of sleep. I wasn't sure how much longer I could continue to do that. I was in the General Studies curriculum in high school and just getting by. College wasn't something I was considering. I was just trying to survive week to week.

CHAPTER 3

GROWING UP FAST

In 1969, exhausted and with the draft breathing down my neck, I decided to join the U.S. Marines rather than wait for the army to come calling. My cousin Joe Vinhais and my friends Tony Pires and Joe Teixeira had joined the marines under the buddy program. My brother-in-law Tony had decided to join the navy rather than wait for the army to come calling. I decided not to wait. For a private, the pay was $107 per month. After taxes, we received $45 every two weeks. However, no one was joining for the money. There was a national draft, so we didn't really have a choice.

My voyage started at the Armed Forces Induction Center in New Haven, Connecticut. The staff was mostly medical personnel, with a few active duty non-commissioned officers (NCO) here and there. They wanted to make sure that recruits were medically fit before they were shipped off. As I recall, all the men there that day, approximately 150 of us, were going into either the army or the marines. There was one sergeant whose command voice suggested he might have been a former drill instructor. When he said move, you moved. They had us line up along the wall of a large room facing the center with our underwear around our ankles. The sergeant called us to a position of attention, which meant facing straight ahead and placing our hands along our sides. This left our genitals exposed. For the first test, the doctor came up to each one of us and checked us for hernias. This

27

entailed each young man turning his head to the side and coughing while the doctor felt under his testicles. I don't know what reaction he was looking for, but apparently everyone passed. The only levity of the day came when the doctor commented that it appeared one of the draftees had wrapped his testicles in cotton. There were a few snickers, but everyone tried hard to keep any laughter under control.

With our underwear back in place, the process resumed. The sergeant with the command voice called out the marine recruits and directed us to a corner of the large room. Once the army recruits had filled in the gaps we had left along the wall, he proceeded with a speech directed at them. Apparently, the Marine Corps recruiters had failed to meet their quota that month. They were seventeen recruits short. He was looking for seventeen army draftees to volunteer to go into the marines. He asked all volunteers to take one step forward. Nothing! He again tried his little speech about how we were all on the same team and we had to help our sister service. The results were the same. Finally, he said, "Okay girls, this is how we are going to do this. I'm going to start on one end and tap every third man. That man will step forward. I will continue the process until we have seventeen volunteers. Do you understand?" Well, to no one's surprise, the marines ended up meeting their quota. We ended up with seventeen recruits who had thought they were going to the army's Fort Dix in New Jersey and ended up writing home from Parris Island, South Carolina. The army recruits were all draftees, so they didn't have much of a choice.

Once we got to Parris Island and they cut our hair, you couldn't tell one guy from another. I couldn't say what the success rate for completion of training was between the army draftees and those of us who had enlisted in the marines. There was a big incentive to stay and graduate with your platoon. Those who lacked motivation or fought the program, found themselves being dropped to another platoon that was two or three weeks behind in the training cycle.

After eight weeks of boot camp at Parris Island, South Carolina, I went through the normal follow-on infantry training at Camp Lejeune, North Carolina, and Camp Pendleton, California, before being shipped off to Vietnam. After putting me through a series of aptitude tests in boot camp, the Marine Corps decided that my skills would be best utilized as a rifleman. I wasn't alone. The Marine Corps reached the same conclusion regarding seventy-eight of the eighty men who had graduated from boot camp with me. The only exceptions were two brothers who had a few years of college. They were trained as administrative clerks.

My sister Linda got married while I was attending infantry training at Camp Lejeune, North Carolina. Getting leave to attend the wedding was out of the question. I had seen others make such requests and be ridiculed by the staff, so I didn't even ask. During the last week at infantry training school, the marines put us through a ten-day field training exercise. This was near the end of July 1969, which coincided with the moon landing. It had rained nonstop for three or four days in North Carolina during that period. I remember sitting in a foxhole in six inches of water, listening to a small transistor radio as the broadcaster explained the images he was seeing on TV. We all listened attentively, thinking how great it would be to see this firsthand rather than listen to the description on the radio.

On our way to Vietnam, we stopped off in Okinawa, Japan, for more briefings on the rules of engagement and country orientation. While there, I got to see both my cousin Joe and my friend Tony. Their unit had been pulled out of Vietnam early, and they were completing the rest of their thirteen-month tour in Okinawa. I had grown up with these guys, but somehow they seemed different. War had changed them. The day after I arrived in Okinawa, I observed something that I will never forget. It was raining, as it often did in Okinawa. There were lines of marines into some of the warehouses on base. The new guys ran from place to place, trying to avoid the rain. The Vietnam returnees just stood there in the rain. They made no effort to stay dry. They had a look in their eyes unlike anything I had ever seen. The eyes appeared dead. No one smiled or joke. No one spoke unless they were addressed directly. These men were changed.

When I arrived in Vietnam, I was assigned to the First Marine Division. From division headquarters, I was sent to the Twenty-Sixth Marine Regiment. This regiment was actually part of the Fifth Marine Division, which had not been activated since World War II. During the Vietnam War, the Marine Corps activated all three of the division's regiments, the Twenty-Sixth, Twenty-Seventh, and Twenty-Eighth, but not the division HQ. Instead, it attached the regiments to the First Marine Division. The Twenty-Sixth Marine Regiment HQ assigned me to the second battalion, and the battalion to H Company. I finally ended up in second platoon, H Co. 2/26. We went from place to place in a two-and-a-half-ton truck called a six-by-six. It was not exactly built for comfort. Some trucks had tarps over the top to keep the rain out; others did not.

My first duty in Vietnam was at a place called Hai Van Pass, guarding Highway 1. It was the primary north–south route along the east coast of South Vietnam. After a month or so, the company traveled further north to Hill 88, also along Highway 1. It is just south of the city of Hue. We had an artillery battery in support. Our mission was to keep Highway 1 open by patrolling the nearby mountains. Our patrols were designed to keep the Viet Cong and North Vietnam regulars from mounting attacks on the highway.

I went on my first ambush a couple of days after our arrival there. I was naturally scared, but I was with some veterans, so I figured I would be okay. The Standard Operating Procedure (SOP) was that we all stayed awake until midnight. After that, we went to 50 percent watch. I was one of the new guys, so I was assigned the middle of three two-hour watches. No one had a wristwatch, or so they said. I was new in Vietnam, so I still had the twenty-dollar Seiko I had bought in Camp Lejeune. The first watch stander asked to borrow it so he would know when to wake me. It was a reasonable request, so I handed over my watch. It seemed like I had just closed my eyes when I felt myself being shaken. "It's your turn for watch." I remember thinking, already! It seemed like I had just lain down, but he showed me the watch, and sure enough, it was 2:00 a.m. At 4:00 a.m. I tried to wake up my relief but I couldn't locate him. That night I learned one of my first lessons, you should always know exactly where your relief is sleeping. It was common practice to roll up in your poncho liner to keep the mosquitoes away. Everyone I shook said, "It's not me." After what seemed like hours, one of the marines got up to pee and I asked him if he knew where my relief was sleeping. He went over and told the marine to get up, and he did. I was sure I had awakened him and he had given me the brush-off. I handed him my watch without thinking. Since he was the last watch, he didn't really need it.

What seemed like fifteen minutes later and while still dark, the squad leader came around, kicking everyone's feet. It was time to break up the ambush and head back to base camp. There was a reason it had seemed like a very long night for me. The first watch stander had moved the watch hands forward after about twenty minutes of his watch. When I figured it out and confronted him, his response was that he was tired and had not wanted to fall asleep on watch. The marine who had replaced me on watch, denied having taken my watch. I never saw my watch again.

Being the new guy in the platoon was getting to be a bigger challenge than I had imagined. Most of the casualties were marines with fewer than ninety days in-country. If you survived the first three months, you had a good chance of making it home. With time, I learned that veterans tended to avoid getting close to new guys because they likely would not be around long. It was nothing personal, simply a self-defense mechanism. Every time you lost a friend, it affected you psychologically. Your inability to focus on the danger around you made you vulnerable and affected your own survival chances.

The obstacles I faced in being accepted as a member of the platoon were exacerbated by the fact that I was Caucasian and an immigrant with a heavy foreign accent. I was the only white guy in the squad. Every other member was either black or of Mexican descent. The racial tension was very high across the board. This was new to me. Although I was a relatively new guy, I found myself often walking point. This was a task normally reserved for marines who had been in-country for six to nine months. The point man had the perilous job of leading the squad, followed by the platoon and the company when operating at the company level. Most of the time, we operated at the platoon level. He had the responsibility for guiding the unit from point A to point B on the map. He was also responsible for detecting booby traps and ensuring he didn't walk the platoon into an ambush. When our platoon brought up the rear, I was always the very last man in the column. When the unit moved at night, in pitch darkness, it was easy to become separated from the rest of your unit.

The first time I walked point, I was given the following advice by my squad leader: "Watch out for booby traps, and don't walk us into any ambushes." Needless to say, I was performing these new duties with upmost caution. A couple of weeks later, I spoke with my squad leader privately about my lack of experience to walk point. His response shocked me a bit. He said, "Listen, asshole, if anybody in this squad is going to get killed, it's going to be you." The message was loud and clear. I was on my own. I kept the exchange to myself.

Unless they were part of a major operation, most platoons operated independently in Vietnam. Your chances of living through the experience often depended on the ability of a twenty-three-year-old second lieutenant to read a map and use a compass. You had to know your position as well as be able to navigate to your objective at all times. Only then, could you use supporting arms should you get in a pickle. Aviation support, artillery and mortars as well as medical evacuation depended in knowing the exact unit location at all times. Platoons were assigned an area of operation, known as an OP. The rule of thumb was you never stay two nights in one spot. The goal was to move and keep the Viet Cong off balance. Standard operating procedures were essentially the following: Platoons had three squads of between ten and thirteen marines. In addition, they had a radioman, and an attached machine-gun (M60) section of three. The squads would rotate on conducting daily patrols and going out to set up ambushes at night. The squad that conducted the patrol would also scout out a place for the other two squads and the platoon headquarters to overnight. It consisted of the platoon commander (usually a second or first lieutenant), the platoon sergeant, a radioman, and a navy corpsman. The army called such corpsmen "medics." The marines do not have medical and religious personnel in their rolls; they are provided by the navy. The whole platoon would leave the old bivouac site (a military term for a place where a military unit stays overnight), with the squad that had conducted the day patrol on the lead. The squad leader of the lead squad would point out the new bivouac location to the platoon sergeant, who would normally be walking directly behind him. At this point, the platoon sergeant would call up the two squad leaders who would remain in the bivouac area and organize the defense while the lead squad continued on to the ambush position they'd picked out earlier in the day. It was important to time the moment the platoon left the old bivouac area. The platoon had to allow itself enough daylight for the platoon headquarters to set up its defenses and for the third squad to set up the fields of fire required by the ambush. However, a platoon did not want to leave with so much daylight that it was telegraphing its movements to the enemy. During one of these ambushes, our squad was itself ambushed on our way to the ambush site. The platoon was late leaving our old bivouac site, and we were rushing and not taking proper security measures as we moved to the ambush site. The squad leader was killed, and we had three other marines wounded. Medical evacuation (medivac) was out of the question. We ended up setting up a perimeter and requesting both illumination and artillery support all night to keep the enemy in check. At first light we cleared out some brush so the medivac helicopter could land to evacuate our casualties. The medivac chopper was escorted by two Cobra gunships to provide security while we loaded up our dead and wounded.

During the months at Hill 88, the platoon received only two MREs (Meals Ready to Eat) per day. One of the things you could usually count on in the Marine Corps was three square meals and a cot. Many of us bitched about the lack of chow. We all lost weight; the calories from two meals per day were just not enough to hump those mountains on a daily basis. I was down to 135 pounds on a 5' 11" frame, down from 160.

In the spring of 1970, the Twenty-Sixth Marine Regiment pulled out of Vietnam. However, the only marines who could return with the regiment were those who had completed ten months of their thirteen months tour. I didn't meet the criteria, so I was transferred to the Seventh Marine Regiment.

I was glad to be joining a new outfit. I was no longer a new guy in country, and I was sure my integration into a new unit would be a lot smoother. I ended up at Company B, First Battalion, Seventh Marines. The first platoon had the biggest need. They had recently walked into an ambush and lost half a dozen marines. There was an opening in the machine-gun squad, so I volunteered. Although I was a rifleman, I fit right in. I had fired the M-60 in training and was very familiar with it. The machine gun team had a gunner, who carried the twenty-five gun and two assistant gunners who carried ammunition and stepped in if the gunner became a casualty. These machine guns put out so much fire power, that they soon draw attention from enemy positions. Consequently, if you want to survive, you fire a few bursts and move, fire and move. I was handed the M-60 machine gun and had the privilege of carrying an extra twenty five pounds. Two one hundred round belts were an extra fifteen pounds. I was now up to forty pounds plus my back pack, water canteens, combat rations, grenade, pop up flares etc. etc. Since I carried the machine gun, I didn't have to carry claymore mines or mortar rounds. We were loaded down.

The regimental and battalion headquarters were in an operating base in the middle of nowhere, called LZ (Landing Zone) Baldy. I know it was in Quam Tri Province, but little else. The goal was to live to scratch off another day in your short-timer's calendar. Everybody had one. Enemy activity appeared to be lower than it had been with my other unit farther north, but we still made frequent contact with the enemy. On one occasion, I was with the main body of the platoon, when we were the target of a mortar attack. Apparently, the location had already been registered for fire. With indirect-fire weapons such as artillery and mortars, you took your best shot, and then you adjusted fires. You either added or subtracted or went left or right of your place of impact. In this case, the very first round landed inside our perimeter. Nobody was that good. The enemy had known we were operating in the area and anticipated our use of the location for an overnight bivouac. We suffered four casualties, mostly from shrapnel, and those men were evacuated the following day. Several of us including me, caught small pieces of shrapnel, but the corpsman simply patched us up, and we stayed with the platoon.

Operations became routine. The platoon would go out for forty-five days and then return to LZ Baldy for three days or so. During this three day period, we constituted the reserve. If one of the battalion units got in trouble, we were flown out to reinforce them. During these three days, we had a standard routine. The very first thing, the platoon was lined up and each marine was given either two beers and a Coke or two Cokes and a beer. Some marines didn't drink but had no trouble exchanging with those who did. The beer cans were wet rather than cold and normally had rusty tops, but this didn't bother the guys who enjoyed a beer. That would be followed by a hot meal, normally consisting of a steak. Another luxury! Marines were allowed to take a shower, a hot one if your platoon was the first to get in. We were also issued new uniforms and boots. Boots sizes were often a problem, but our platoon sergeant was pretty good at getting us what we needed. Uniforms and boots would literally rot off our bodies. It was unbelievable what six weeks in the jungle would do to a set of utilities. We carried only the set we wore. Our packs were heavy, so we carried only the essentials. The only luxury we allowed ourselves was a couple of extra pairs of socks. In addition to our weapons and ammunition, we carried grenades, claymore mines, mortar shells, illumination pop-ups, and of course, food and water. The average back pack exceeded sixty pounds.

During our three days in the rear, we didn't have to stand night watch, but there were plenty of working parties during the day. After morning formation, we tried to make ourselves scarce. If you got caught hanging around the tent, you would soon be recruited by the company gunny to go burn the latrines using diesel fuel. It was not a pleasant smell. Although outdoor movies were shown nightly, most marines opted to catch up on much-needed sleep. We also trained. All ammunition had a shelf life. Much of it got dirty as we rolled around in the mud. We would either fire it off while in the rear or blow it up with C-4 plastic explosives. We were always issued new ammo before we went out again. During one of those firing exercises, my M-60 machine gun jammed, as it often did during normal operations. I carried one hundred rounds in the gun pouch and another hundred or two across my chest, Poncho Villa style, for easy access. Those rounds picked up sand and dirt and made the gun susceptible to jamming. As I tried to clear the blockage, the round cooked off— that is, fired—due to the heat generated in the chamber, and I ended up with gunpowder burns in both of my corneas. As a result, I was medically evacuated out of Vietnam. First, I was taken to the USNS *Comfort* off the coast of Vietnam, and from there I was sent to the naval hospital in Guam. In Guam, the ophthalmologist decided that I needed at least another two months to recuperate fully. He gave me two options: stay in Guam until I was fully recovered, and then go back to Vietnam, or he could send me back to the United States where I could recover somewhere near my home town. The doctor asked me if I had a preference, I couldn't believe my ears. I had had enough of Vietnam. I was sent to the Saint Albans Naval Hospital in Queens, New York, to recover near my home in Connecticut.

After recovering from my eye injuries, I returned to active duty at Camp Lejeune, North Carolina. My stay in Camp Lejeune was short-lived. Within forty-eight hours of reporting to the Eighth Marine Regiment, I was on a plane headed to Guantanamo Bay, Cuba, where I would be part of the infantry company that provided security along the fence between the US base and the country of Cuba. While in Guantanamo Bay, I was promoted to corporal. After six months in Cuba, I returned to Camp Lejeune and was assigned to A Company, First Battalion, Sixth Marine Regiment.

The battalion was training for a six-month deployment to the Caribbean Sea. I joined the unit in March 1971. My platoon commander, First Lieutenant Andrew Broadstone, nominated me to attend the noncommissioned officers (NCO) school course—because I was a Vietnam returnee, I assumed. It was a six-week course in a remote part of Camp Lejeune. There were approximately sixty of us assigned to the course. During the orientation portion, I learned that the honor man, or the person who finished first in the class, would be meritoriously promoted to sergeant. The war in Vietnam was winding down and promotions were slow. I saw a great opportunity to get around the promotion backlog. The course would consist of academics, leadership, and military skills. I made up my mind to go for the number one spot.

As part of our daily evaluation, one of the three instructors would come by the barracks to inspect the general area and to check to see if our beds were made properly. We were required to make our beds with twelve inches of the bottom sheet showing, plus a six-inch fold of the top sheet, for a total of eighteen inches of white. A ruler was used to ensure compliance. The bed had to be tight enough so that the instructors could, and often would, bounce a quarter on it. The instructors inspected daily, but every Friday morning, everyone stood by his bed with his wall locker open for inspection. Wake-up time was 5:00 a.m. We had to shower, shave, and so on and be outside in formation for physical training by 5:45 a.m. Time was tight. Sometimes one of the instructors would come by and inspect our living areas, which included our beds, while we were out for our physical fitness routine. I decided to get an extra blanket and pillow and sleep on the concrete floor. I had a car that I had bought for three hundred dollars, and I kept the extra blanket and pillow in the trunk of the car, which was parked in a nearby parking lot.

By the end of the course, I thought I had done pretty well. When the finalists were announced, we were told there was a tie for second. That took some air out of my sails. Finally, they announced the number one in the course. When academics, military skills, and leadership scores were added up, I had the highest average in the class. My hard work and sacrifice had paid off. This also gave me confidence that I could accomplish something if I set my mind to it. In two years in the Marine Corps, I had gone from private to sergeant. My company and battalion commanders attended the ceremony. I went back to my platoon with a little spring in my step and new sergeant stripes on my sleeves.

The end of our unit's Caribbean deployment coincided with the approaching end of my enlistment contract. As the platoon was taking a break during one of the many deployment exercises, Lieutenant Broadstone approached me. My first thought was that he was going to provide me with some observations on my squad's performance during the just-completed exercise. I was surprised when he sat down and asked me about my future plans instead. He asked if I planned to remain in the corps. I told him that it was highly unlikely. As we continued to talk, he said, "Have you given any thought to college? I think you are college material." That was the first time anyone had said that to me. No one in my family had ever gone to college. However, the more I thought about it, the more appealing the idea became to me. He had planted the seed, and now I couldn't stop thinking about it. I had many doubts. I hadn't spent much time with the books in high school because of my full-time job. I had just spent three years in the Marine Corps, away from academics. Could I do college work? Could I compete with kids fresh out of high school?

CHAPTER 4

MY COLLEGE YEARS

I left the Marine Corps at the end of my enlistment contract and returned home to Connecticut. My first task was to get a job. A week after I got home, I had a job in construction. The work was hard, but the pay was fair. I couldn't get the idea of attending college out of my mind. I was also engaged to be married, to my first girlfriend. We had written each other regularly while I was on active duty, and she had kept track of our contemporaries who had gotten married. She was my age, but she sounded like she was afraid of becoming an old maid. Her parents were strict. I think she saw marriage as a means to finally live. We were not allowed to date until we had a wedding date set. We were married in June 1972. Once married, we rented my parents' upstairs apartment. I had saved enough money to fully furnish the apartment, and we had worked out a fair rent with my parents.

I had decided that just as in high school, I could work and go to school. I had also decided that my best chance for success, from both a financial and an academic standpoint, was to attend the local community college. The Veterans Administration's college tuition assistance program was a great financial help. My goal was to graduate in four years. While working a forty-hour week in construction, I registered for four classes at night, 6:00–10:00 p.m., Monday through Thursday. Halfway through my first semester, I was doing well in three of the courses, but it had become clear that I wasn't going to pass algebra. While in high school, I'd had no plans to go to college, so algebra hadn't been required. I just didn't have the background in math to walk into college algebra. The teacher suggested I drop the class and take a "withdraw" rather than a failing grade. I took her advice, but now I would have to take two classes in summer school to remain on track to graduate in four years.

I was so focused on work and school that I failed to realize my marriage was in real trouble. My wife was unhappy because she felt neglected. She had wanted to get married so she could finally be out of her parents' strict control. She wanted to go out; she wanted to live. But I was working a forty-hour week in construction and spending every spare minute either in class or studying. The way I saw it, I had to work to cover the bills. I had also made a decision to attend college. Our lack of quality time together was a short-term sacrifice in my view. My decision to join the college's soccer team exacerbated my marriage difficulties. In retrospect, I should have seen this coming. The coach was tolerant with me because he was aware of my situation. I went to practice on Fridays only and to the games on Saturdays.

By December 1972, my marriage was on the verge of breaking up. Although I had been able to juggle school and work in high school, it was becoming obvious that I could not add marriage to the equation and make it work. I had to work, and I had also made a conscious decision to attend college. I discussed the matter with my wife. I asked her to hang in there. She was adamant—I should either drop out of school or lighten my academic load and graduate in six years rather than four. I saw that as a slippery slope. Therefore, I had to choose between my marriage and attending college. After thinking long and hard, I made the most difficult decision of my young life. I chose to continue my college education. Six months after we married, our marriage was over, and she was back home, living with her parents. The divorce was very hard on both of our families. The divorce was not finalized for another year. Shortly thereafter, working through the local diocese we had our marriage annulled. She remained in Connecticut and I went back to active duty after college. We never spoke again. She later remarried and had a daughter. She passed away from colon cancer at forty-nine.

I took a full load (fifteen credits) during my first spring semester and did quite well academically. I was six credits short from the fall semester, so I had to make up those credits during summer school. The courses I needed were offered only in the morning and midday, so I had to find an evening summer job. I found a job working from 4:00 p.m. to midnight. I was told the job involved mixing chemicals. I could see myself in a white smock with some test tubes. Imagine my surprise when I was confronted with eighty-pound bags of asbestos material. I had to dump these bags into a large mixer and add a series of chemicals to the powder. The product was processed into car brake pads. The job was piecework, so the faster I worked, the more money I made. After a break-in period of one week, I was on my own. There was great demand, so the company was running three shifts. It needed all the product we could produce, and the company pressured employees to work overtime. It was possible to produce twelve hours of work in eight hours. I had to turn the mixers over to the new shift at midnight. However, despite having finished twelve hours' worth of work by midnight, I had to stay in the factory until 4:00 a.m. I had a summer class that started at 8:00 a.m., so I did not get much sleep. Consequently, I limited my overtime to Friday and Saturday nights.

In the spring of 1973, a problem arose. I was now living in the upstairs apartment of my parents' two-family home. My dad did not mind my going to college during the winter months, when the construction industry laid off most of their employees, but he expected me to be his ride to work during the summer months. I tried to explain to him that I needed two summer school classes and would not be able to provide him with a ride. There was some tension at home for a couple of weeks. Finally, my mother approached me one day. She said, "If you want to go to college, go to college. Leave your father to me." That was the last I heard from my dad about the subject.

During the summer of 1973, my brother Antonio (Toze) was killed in a car accident. He had been going through the normal adolescent growing pains. Earlier in the year, he had forged my parents' signatures on a note authorizing him to quit school at the age of sixteen. Once my parents found out about it, they revoked it.

My sister Linda was living in West Hartford, Connecticut. My brother-in-law Tony, was working for the state of Connecticut as a civil engineer in Hartford. My mother (as all parents do) thought that the kids Toze hung around with were the primary cause of his behavioral problems. My sister was able to get my brother into a Catholic private school in Hartford during the spring of 1973. Away from his friends, my brother managed to stay out of trouble, though his grades left a lot to be desired. Two weeks after the end of school year and back home, my brother was killed in an automobile accident. Apparently, his nineteen-year-old friend, the driver, had been drinking. My brother was riding shotgun in the front seat without a seatbelt. The car apparently skidded off the road and hit a tree. The car rolled over, ejecting my brother and landing on top of him. The whole family was devastated. My brother was dead at the age of sixteen before he had a chance to live his life. My mother had given birth to nine children, and we were down to five.

In the fall of 1973, I quit my summer night job and enrolled in school full-time. I was now back on track to graduate in four years. The fall semester went extremely well academically. Things were going well sports-wise. I managed to lead my soccer team in scoring despite playing center midfield. I was not happy because, I wasn't playing my normal forward position, but the coach insisted midfield was where I could best help the team.

In the spring of 1974, I graduated from the local community college with a B+ average. I had applied to, and been accepted at the University of Connecticut, and I went as far as registering for the following fall semester. However, my soccer skills had caught the attention of the Fairfield University coach. One day I got a call from him, asking me to meet him at the athletic director's office the following morning, with a copy of my official transcript. When I arrived at that meeting, he asked about my plans for the fall semester. I told him about registering for classes at the University of Connecticut. He asked if I would like to attend Fairfield, and I told him I would love to. Fairfield might have been one of the newest Jesuit universities in the country, but it soon became one of the best universities in the Northeast. However, I was a veteran who was paying his own way. I didn't think I could afford the tuition. The coach said that he had been looking for a case like mine to take to the athletic director. Presently, the vast majority of the school's sports scholarship money was going into the basketball program. It was time to spread it around. I wanted full tuition but would settle for half. Two days later, he called me. He told me I had the money and said to go by the admissions office to take care of the necessary paperwork.

Later that summer, I attended the United States Marine Corps Platoon Leaders Class. I had applied for the program that spring when the Marine Corps officer recruiters came by the junior college. The program consisted of two six-week training sessions at Quantico, Virginia. If you successfully completed both sessions of the program, you were commissioned a second lieutenant in the United States Marine Corps after college graduation. One of the program's appealing aspects was that I was not committed until I graduated. Returning to the Marine Corps as a commissioned officer was an option I had long considered. The marines ran two summer classes, one from early June to the middle of July and a second one, the one I was attending, from the middle of July to the end of August. I had the same doubts about becoming an officer in the marines that I'd had about my ability to do college work. I had been exposed to some great officers in the Marine Corps. One in particular, Lieutenant Broadstone, had been responsible for my decision to attend college. He had seen qualities in me that I had not recognized in myself. I never ran into him again, although he spent twenty years on active duty. When I looked him up a few years ago, I discovered that he had passed away in 2014, in northern Virginia. Apparently, he had taught school there for years after he retired. I never had an opportunity to tell him how he had influenced my life.

The first six-week program was challenging. The heat and humidity in Quantico during the months of July and August were brutal. The program incorporated rigorous physical fitness activity into the mornings while focusing on academics during the afternoons. The marines had a program called "drop on request." Psychological pressure was applied at all times. The object was to weed out those who were unable to make the grade. Instructors would remind candidates that they could request to be dropped, and a fair number did just that. Officer Candidates School covered the same three areas as NCO school, but at a much more advanced level : academics, military skills, and leadership. The information covered in each of those subjects was obviously different, but the program worked the same with one exception: peer evaluations. You had control over how well you did in academics and military skills. You could get 100 percent in every test, shoot expertly with the rifle and pistol, and show that you were able to read a map and use a compass. However, you had little or no control over your leadership grade. Your instructors and your peers evaluated your leadership qualities. Every officer candidate rated every other member of the unit numerically. Not everyone was asked to return the following year. I went in with the goal of doing the best I could, hoping that in the end, it would be good enough for me to return next year. In the end, I finished second in my class. I was a little surprised and greatly encouraged.

In the fall of 1974, I enrolled at Fairfield University. I was surprised to find there were five other students enrolled in the United States Marine Corps Platoon Leader's Class (PLC). They were, Robert Cypher, Larry Sweeney, Mike Sullivan, Steve Butera and Rick Schwartz. Robert Cypher was commissioned with me in 1976, but went to law school, and didn't report for active duty until three years later. As an attorney, he joined the judge advocate corps (JAG). He left active duty after his contract obligation, but remained active in the Marine Corps reserve until he retired after twenty years of total service. I ended up running into Bob, at our forty-fifth college reunion in October 2022. I was my first class reunion. My years on active duty and the subsequent twelve years I spent in Portugal made it difficult for me to attend. I was glad to see Bob hadn't changed much after all of these years. I was also very pleased to learn he is a district judge in the state of New York.

The others were commissioned a year later. It was quiet a coincidence that while writing this book, I received a card in the mail from Larry Sweeney. Apparently he saw my name mentioned in the college's quarterly news letter as an attendee at our college reunion. He decided to Google my name, and it turns out we live in the same town in Florida. We are probably four miles apart as the crow flies. Yet, we hadn't seen each other since I dropped him off at Norton Air Force Base in California, to catch a military flight to Okinawa, Japan forty-four years ago. Larry served eight year on active duty, before leaving the Corps and join the active Marine Corps Reserve. I'm not surprised that both Bob and Larry decide to remain involved with the Marine Corps Reserve after leaving active duty. There really is a lot to the saying "once a Marine, always a Marine". Once you internalize Marine Corps values, they are difficult to leave behind. It was great to see him and his wife Nancy. Larry and I were both members of the school's soccer team. We hope to see a lot more of each other in the future and relive some of our college days' experiences. I pretty much lost track of the other members of the PLC at program at Fairfield, after I entered active duty.

Academics at Fairfield were much more demanding there, at the community college. Our soccer season was during the fall semester. I was the only one on the team getting financial aid. The team wasn't very good, and it was a long season. I finished the fall semester of my junior year with a 2.8 grade point average. I was disappointed with my GPA, so I decided to quit my part-time job and focus on academics.

My grades improved gradually. I finished my degree in the top half of my class. I wrapped up my last semester of my senior year with a 3.5 Grade Point Average (GPA).

In the summer of 1975, I returned to Quantico for the second portion of the U.S. Marines' officer candidate program. I had a better idea of what to expect this year. I was strong in academics and military skills. I decided to focus on the one area I had least control over. Having spent three years on active duty, I had gone through dozens and dozens of inspections. I pretty much knew where the inspectors would look when inspecting a uniform or a rifle. As a result, I seldom got called for any discrepancies during our weekly Saturday morning inspections. I started giving some of my peer's tips on how to clean a rifle. I soon had many of my peers lined up for me to inspect their weapons. Often, this would go on until lights went out on Friday nights. This gesture on my part didn't go unnoticed by my peers. At the end of the six-week course, I was the class honor man.

During early spring of my senior year, the head of the Marine Corps Officer Procurement Office, Brigadier General Richard Shultz, visited Fairfield University. He had come to present me with the Commandant's Leftwich Trophy. It was presented in recognition of outstanding leadership demonstrated during my Officer Candidates School. The university president held a small reception for the event, and my family was invited. A picture of the presentation appeared in the local Sunday paper. My parents were very proud. They had been unsure about my decision to accept a commission in the marines after graduation, but I could tell that this event brought them around.

March 1964, one month after we arrived in the
United States. From Left to right, Micky, Linda,
Toze, Mario and Carlos with Rui in front

With Patricia age 4 in Hawaii 1989

Getting ready for Desert Storm 1990

Patricia with Grandma Candida in Chaves, Portugal 1997

Thanksgiving at my house 2014

Patricia's birthday 2014

Rotary Presentation in Chaves 2017

Marine Corps Birthday in 1994, with some
of my Virginia friends from Chaves

With Trish and my grandson Walker Chritmas 2019

My first picture, taken for my passport 1963

Basic School Class 2-76 classmates

Christmas 1992

Desert Storm 1991

Patricia's college graduation at FSU 2007

Grandpa with Walker 2021

With my wife Wanda, within the walls of
the Castel of Obidos, Portugal

My wife Wanda and I Christmas 2018

On our wedding day, August 30, 2019

My machinegun Team 1970 Vietnam. The author is in the middle

My dad as a recruit in the Portuguese Army 1943

My father in 1963, at age 44

My mother in 1963, at age 38

With my daughter Trish at Christmas 2017

My wife Wanda and my daughter Patricia 2018

With Liam, Jacob and Katie 2014

With Chritina during her visit to FL in 2014

Presentation of the Leftwich Trophy by General
Shultzs at Fairfield University. December 1975

With the Commandant of the Marine Corps,
General Mundy, May 1995

My brother Toze age 15, 1972

My parents Circa 1968

My shadow box with my awards. Presented
to me upon my Retirement

My daughter Carla after I returned from
my pilgramige to Fatima 1983

Grandpa holding Lia when she is three days old

With my parents in Chaves, Portugal in 1983

The Roman Bridge in Chaves built between 74-104 AD

Commanding Officer of MACS-1 in 1995

Picture from my Tour at Naval Space Command 1999

The Mameluke sword displayed in my office. It's
worn by all Marine Corps officers. It was a gift from
my father the day I was commissioned in 1976

All Marine Soccer Team 1981

CHAPTER 5

BACK IN THE CORPS

I was commissioned a second lieutenant in the United States Marine Corps on May 29, 1976. Two weeks later, on June 16, I reported to the Basic School in Quantico, Virginia. The Basic School was a twenty-six-week school that every marine officer goes through, regardless of what he subsequently does in the corps. It doesn't matter if you are going to be a pilot, an attorney, an administrative officer, or an infantry officer; everyone goes through the same initial training. You learn everything you needed to know to be an officer. You received instructions on everything from the Uniform Code of Military Justice, to how to lead an infantry patrol to calling in artillery, air support and naval gunfire support.

The marine corps has two types of officers: reserve and regular officers. A reserve officer comes in under a contract of normally three years. Regular officers serve under an open contract. It is said they serve at the pleasure of the president. Until approximately 1990, officers coming out of the service academies, such as West Point, the Naval Academy, and the Air Force Academy, were commissioned as regular officers. Since the number of regular officers in each service is set by law, obtaining a regular commission is very competitive. I was aware that officers who finished in the top 5 percent of the Basic School would be offered regular commissions. Since I had decided to make the Marine Corps a career, it was important to obtain a regular commission as soon as possible.

We had a class of 250 officers divided into five platoons. Each platoon had fifty young second lieutenants led by a captain. The five platoons comprised a company led by a major. We would spend twenty-six weeks together, so we got to know each other pretty well. Five percent of 250 are 12.5. That meant I had to finish in the top thirteen. Furthermore, I had to take into consideration that some of the service academy members in our company already had regular commissions. In the event some of them finished near the top of the class as they inevitably would, they would take up some of those very limited spots. Regulations didn't make exception for the spots taken up by the regular officers. Instead of thirteen, we may end up with just ten or so.

Approximately twenty weeks into the twenty –six weeks training cycle, they posted a list of our class standing. Those of us who were not already designated to attend flight school or Judge Advocate School, had to pick a military occupational specialty. The Marine Corps broke the class up into thirds and also divided the number of openings in each of the military occupational specialties (MOS) into thirds. This way, the talent would be divided across the board, and the Marine Corps could avoid having the top third of the class in the most popular MOS and the bottom of the class in the less popular specialties. I was ranked in ninth place out of the 250 officer students. I could have picked any MOS I wanted. I was intrigued by, and finally settled on air defense control, but I couldn't find a lot of information on the MOS. There were no officers from this field at the Basic School from whom I could get information. I knew one thing: I'd had my share of infantry during my days in Vietnam. I was told that the three-month follow-on course in air defense would be challenging, and it was.

In retrospect, I should have picked artillery or combat engineer.

This was the first of several occasions where a mentor would have come in handy over the course of my career. *You don't know what you don't know.* I would often use this phrase when counseling young officers as I became more senior. Officers who did not pick what the Marine Corps referred to as combat arms were penalized in their leadership grade. In the end, I finished ninth in the overall class of 241, but was rated fifth in leadership by my platoon commander. This brought my overall ranking down to ninth. Despite having lower academic averages, all four of the officers rated over me went into either infantry or artillery. All five of the captains which led each of the platoons plus the company commander were infantry officers. Of course, it is also possible that my MOS selection had nothing to do with my leadership rating. The bottom line was that I had achieved what I had set out to do: I had finished in the top 5 percent and was offered a regular commission. The paperwork caught up to me after I got to my first squadron about six months later. I was extremely happy to see my parents and my sisters Linda and Micky at the graduation ceremony. Incidentally, they were pregnant, Linda with her second, Shawn, and Micky with her first, Jason.

I graduated from the Basic School on December 19, 1976. I had orders to report to Air Defense Intercept School in Twenty-nine Palms, California, on January 2, 1977. I loaded up everything I owned in the back of my recently acquired Datsun 280Z and drove across the country. I had few possessions other than my recently acquired uniforms. The drive was uneventful with the exception of a snowstorm in Flagstaff, Arizona. I had planned the trip in advance, and Flagstaff was going to be an overnight stay anyway. It snowed all night. When I got in my car the next day to continue my trip west, the going was slow and treacherous. Just as I decided to pull over and wait for the snow to lighten up a bit, a snowplow came by. I decided to get behind the snowplow and ride it out. I got to Twenty-nine Palms on New Year's Eve. I checked in with the school's executive officer, who in a very casual way told me how happy he was to see me. It seemed the duty officer assigned for New Year's Day had to go on emergency leave. Welcome aboard! I was told that I should spend a few hours with the duty officer that night, so I could read and become familiar with the pertinent base orders before I assumed duty the following morning.

The class started as scheduled on January 2, with fifteen officers. We were already assigned a squadron to report to after graduation. I was assigned to the Marine Air Control Squadron at Camp Pendleton, California. Our mission was to provide air-to-air intercept control training for the three fighter squadrons of Marine Aircraft Group 11 (MAG-11) stationed in El Toro, California. We would develop proficiency as ground control intercept (GCI) controllers while the pilots developed proficiency in intercepting and conducting what were called "dog fights" with other aircraft. The F-4 Phantoms would engage the much smaller F-5s which was similar in size and simulated the tactics of the Soviet MIG-21. More experienced controllers would supervise each new controller until he was sure the new controller could handle the job. There were a series of tests and exercises to go through before a controller was designated fully qualified. A GCI controller would control either two (section) or four (division) twenty-five-million-dollar aircraft. The Marine Corps policy was to assign primarily officers as GCI controllers, although we had some senior enlisted personnel working by our sides.

Shortly after arriving at Camp Pendleton, I enrolled in a master's program offered on base by Pepperdine University. I had concluded that if I was going to make the Marine Corps a career, a bachelor's degree might no longer be enough. I needed at least a master's degree. I have never been a procrastinator. There is never a time like the present to get something done. Classes were from 5:00–10:00 p.m. on Fridays, 8:00 a.m.–5:00 p.m. on Saturdays, and 8:00 a.m.–1:00 p.m. on Sundays every other weekend. I normally spent my off weekends researching and writing papers. This didn't leave much time for a social life, but I was single and would never have that flexibility again once I got married. After passing an eight hour comprehensive exam covering material from all twelve courses, I was awarded an MA in Human Resources Management/Personnel Management from Pepperdine University in April 1979.

In February 1978, my younger brother Carlos got married and invited me to be his best man. During my time in Connecticut, I ran into a girl who was from our village in Portugal. We went on a few dates, but my mother was not too keen on our relationship. After my ten days annual leave, I returned to southern California. Despite just a few dates, we decided to get married. I was ready to settle down, and with so much in common, what could go wrong? She remained in Connecticut. The following summer, we met in Portugal and married in our hometown. My parents did not attend. We returned to Southern California together and lived in a house I had purchased the year before.

She got pregnant during our honeymoon. Thirty-six weeks later, Carla was born. Complications ensued from the beginning. Our daughter was born with congenital glaucoma, a high intraocular pressure that affects the optic nerve and can cause blindness if left untreated for long. The pediatrician at the Camp Pendleton naval hospital, where she was born, caught her condition during her post birth examination. Carla had nine different surgical procedures in her first twelve months of life. She saw some of the best ophthalmologists in the country, from Southern California to San Francisco to Massachusetts General Hospital and Yale. When she was three, we discovered that in addition to having glaucoma, Carla was also functioning in the severely autistic range scale.

My wife and I were overwhelmed by the challenge we faced. Faith had always played an important role in my life. Whenever I had found myself in a particularly tight spot in Vietnam, I would often pray to Sao Caetano. He is a popular patron saint near our village in Portugal, and I had often heard my mother pray to him. During these trying times, I made a promise to visit the sanctuary, say a few prayers, and make a small monetary donation. I made a point of fulfilling my promise the very first time I visited Portugal after I returned from Vietnam.

I now found myself in a similar spot, and I turned to God for help and strength. More precisely, I prayed to Our Lady of Fatima, the patron saint of Portugal, to intercede with God on my behalf. I promised that if Carla's eyesight was saved, I would make a pilgrimage of 270 miles, from my village in northern Portugal to Fatima. In addition, I would do it to coincide with the anniversary of the apparition of the Virgin Mary on the thirteenth of May 1917. In 1983, with Carla's vision stabilized, I took five weeks of annual leave from my unit in Southern California and set off for Portugal to fulfill my promise.

Spring in Portugal that year was cold and wet. Having picked up a small backpack and a pair of well-worn running shoes, I left the village and walked to the nearby town of Chaves, where my parents now resided. I was making the trip alone. Years later, while I was living there after military retirement, I found out that this was a fairly popular pilgrimage. Small groups form up and travel together. Since I was visiting on annual leave, I was not aware of these groups. I don't even know if there were any such groups at the time. The next day, I left Chaves and headed south toward Vila Real, forty miles away. I made it thirty-five miles and then got a taxi and had the driver take me back to Chaves. I had placed my well-worn running shoes in the washing machine and the dryer before leaving home. I had wanted them nice and clean. The problem was that the dryer had shrunk them. I now had two blisters the size of a fifty-cent piece on each of my heels. I had to decide whether I should continue the trip or give up and try another year. After giving the subject much thought, I decided that I had come too far to give up at this point. However, I also realized that if the blisters got infected, the decision would be made for me.

The next morning, I pierced and drained the blisters, cut a big hole in the back of both my running shoes, and headed off. I called a taxi and had the driver drop me off at the place I had stopped the day before. It was a miserable, cold, wet, and windy day. I made other thirty-plus miles that day and then waved down a taxi driver and had him take me to the nearest town. There I found a bed and breakfast, which the Portuguese call a *pensao*, and got a room for the night. After a good dinner and a good night's sleep, I was ready to resume my trip. In the morning, I checked the blisters, put on a clean pair of socks, and resumed my journey. I followed this routine for the eight days it took me to complete the 270-mile trip. I walked most of the trip alone. As I got closer to Fatima, I came across small groups making the same journey, but I found that I made better time walking by myself. As I got closer to Fatima, I found medical aid stations along the sides of the road. The staff was friendly and I would often stop to get my blisters cleaned and bandaged. Luckily, they never got infected.

As I got within a few days' walking of Fatima, I saw large groups of pilgrims congregating in the center of small towns as evening approached. The locals would come up to the groups and take them to their homes for a meal and a place to sleep. One person would come up and say, "I can take two"; another would take three or four. I had means and always paid for my meals and lodging. However, I was touched by the locals' gestures toward complete strangers. All that mattered was that they were pilgrims on a journey of faith.

I arrived in Fatima on the twelfth of May. After settling in and having a nice dinner, I attended something very special. The square at the foot of the cathedral and the small chapel where the statue of the Virgin is kept holds close to a million people. On the evening of May 12, after the rosary, there was a procession of the statue of Our Lady of Fatima around the square. The faithful were handed wax candles, which they lit, and sang "Ave Maria" as the procession made its way around the square. It was a truly moving experience and worth the sacrifice of my journey. The next day, I got up and attended the open door mass in the square along with close to a million other persons. I left feeling that my prayers had been answered.

Over time, Carla ended up losing the vision in her right eye, which was always the more problematic of the two. She did, however, maintain enough vision in her left eye to get around. She needs help around stairs. Depth perception is a problem for individuals with single vision. Her severe autism is something for which there is no cure. She is nonverbal, but her remaining eyesight has allowed her to be ambulatory.

In 1979, the Marine Corps sent me to Okinawa, Japan, for a one-year unaccompanied tour. I was promoted to captain while there. My wife went back to Connecticut to stay near family and friends. She had to deal with Carla's situation alone. I tried to help and found myself writing letters to doctors and the military's medical insurance company (TRICARE) from my tent in South Korea.

In the spring of 1984, I was selected to attend the Amphibious Warfare School in Quantico, VA. It's a nine month school, designed to instruct Captains with 6-9 years of service how to conduct warfare. Many will leave the school and become company commanders. Those who had the opportunity to command a company before attending school will end up going back to a battalion staff. The course is designed to coincide with the children's academic school year. It goes from August to the end of May. Most mid level Captains have small school age children by this time in their carrier, so the timing is designed to minimize the disruption the move causes a family. The class is composed of sixteen groups of fifteen Marine Corps captains for a total of 240, with the widest mix possible of military occupational specialties. In addition to the formal classroom instruction, we spent many hours in classrooms with just the fifteen men groups. The goal was to share experiences and learn from each other. I thought I had been assigned to a great group from the beginning, but when

I look back at the career of some of my classmates, the results are beyond anything anyone us could have predicted. On average, you can expect one general officer to come out of a class of 240 captains. In our group of fifteen alone, three reached general officer rank. One subsequently became Assistant Commandant of the Marine Corps, Commandant of the Marine Corps, Commander-in-Chief Allied Forces in Afghanistan and later Chairman Joint Chiefs of Staff. In the long and illustrious history of the United States Marine Corps, no officer has ever achieved this distinction. There was one additional four star general that came out of our class. I knew him well, and you couldn't find a nicer guy. As it turned out, our class had not one, but four general officers. Two distinguished themselves by achieving four star rank. I became a better officer and better person, for having the honor of engaging in discussions and learning from these outstanding leaders.

In April 1985, while I was going through the Amphibious Warfare School in Quantico, Virginia, our daughter Patricia was born. On our way back to Southern California, we decided to take a detour through our hometown of Bridgeport, Connecticut, to baptize her in the company of family and friends. We moved into our residence in Carlsbad, California, and settled in. Carla returned to her old school. Despite the many problems we encountered, it was comforting to know we were dealing with people who were familiar with her case. It was a trade-off: In order to keep Carla in the same school, I had a ninety-minute commute each way to work. I was out of the house at 5:30 a.m. and would normally get home around 7:30 p.m. While at the helicopter base in Tustin, California, I was the squadron operations officer. Later, I was promoted to major and took over as the squadron executive officer.

In 1988, I was transferred to Marine Air Control Squadron 2 in Oahu, Hawaii, as the squadron executive officer. The commanding officer was going through a very contentious divorce, and it was affecting his ability to lead the squadron. After a year on the job, I asked to be reassigned and ended up in the operations section of the Third Marines Infantry Regiment. After a year there, I was assigned as the First Marine Brigade as the War Plans Officer. Two weeks after I took over this assignment, Iraq invaded Kuwait. First Marine Brigade was part of the contingency plan to defend that part of the world. The aviation units would join the Third Marine Aircraft Wing out of El Toro, California, while the infantry and logistics units would join the First Marine Division out of Camp Pendleton, California. The brigade headquarters would remain behind. My job was to get everyone embarked and out of town. I left on the last airplane.

About five minutes after the large C-5 aircraft took off, a large bird was ingested into the inner left engine of the aircraft. The aircraft was heavily loaded with three CH-46 helicopters and approximately 200 Marines with all of their combat gear. There was no way we could take a chance in making the trip with just three engines. We had to return to base, but first we had to dump the vast majority of the thousands of pounds of jet fuel we had in our tanks. If the pilot tried to land with that much weight, he would likely blow all the tires and collapse the landing gear. First, we had to go way out into the pacific to dump the JP-5 jet fuel. From our altitude, most of the fuel would evaporate before it hit the salt water; however, any fuel that reached the sea had to be out far enough so that it did not reach the Hawaii beaches. That wouldn't be good for tourism. It took the ground crew about twelve hours to move the load we were carrying to another aircraft. Meanwhile we cooled our heals inside the terminal. Many of the troops tried to nap, but there was an underlying feeling of tension. We were heading off to war and none of us knew quiet what to expect on the other end. Once the cargo was loaded, we were on our way again. I didn't even call home during the twelve hours we waited at Hickam Airfield. I had said my goodbyes that morning, and calling and making my family aware of the incident would just worry them.

During the Gulf War, I was part of a Marine Corps contingency team at Central Air Force. Our job was to ensure the integration of Marine Corps aviation into the overall air campaign via the air tasking order (ATO). If it wasn't on the ATO, it wouldn't fly. The hours were long and pressure-packed, but we were led by an outstanding marine colonel named Joseph Robbin. Colonel Robbin was the former commanding officer of Marine Air Control Group 38 in El Toro, California. I had worked for him briefly while in the operations shop at the group headquarters and had enjoyed greatly. After the war, I was awarded the Navy Commendation Medal for work in support of marine operations during the overall air campaign. The secretary of the navy usually awards this medal, but in this case, the task was delegated to the three-star marine forces commander. A copy of the citation is included as appendix 1. On my way back to Hawaii, I was able to stop by Portugal and see my parents before departing for my next duty station.

CHAPTER 6
DREAM ASSIGNMENT

Shortly before I took over as the Brigade's War Plans Officer, I had received a call from Headquarters Marine Corps. I was told there was a job opening for a Marine Corps exchange officer with the Brazilian Marine Corps. The position required Portuguese language skills, which I possessed. Was I interested? The job would not become available until the following summer, but they had to identify someone now because the nominee would have to attend Department of Defense Language School in Monterey, California. I didn't have to think twice. I said yes. In retrospect, maybe I should have given this decision a little more thought.

Once I returned from the Gulf War, it was time to go. We were going as a family, consequently we had to get a medical officer to sign off on all of us. Here we hit a glitch; the medical officer wouldn't sign off on Carla. I had two choices: go alone and send the family back to Connecticut, or call the monitor and pull out. If I made the latter choice, I would be putting the monitor in a difficult situation because of the one-year language training requirement. I talked with my wife, and we decided to buy a house in Connecticut where we both had family, and where she and the children would stay while I went to Brazil alone. The benefit of hindsight being what it is, today I would have made a different decision. I mean, the duty was great professionally. The accommodations were also very good. Rio de Janeiro can be a dangerous place to live. Crime is a huge problem. The local U.S Consulate has to approve the living accommodations. They had a list of apartments which they had pre approved. Incoming personnel picked one based on their family size and a rent the fell within their government allowance. I picked a three bedroom apartment on the beach in the suburb of Leblon. It was more space than I needed, but it was within my budget. I had a special travel budget to visit Brazilian Marine Corps detachments called *agrupamentos* located throughout the country. Brazil is a country the size of the contiguous United States. My job was to be a goodwill ambassador from the United States Marine Corps with our counterparts in Brazil. These visits were normally comprised of a guided tour of their facilities, followed by an hour or so briefing by me to the battalion officers. I had the discretion of selecting the topic, but they knew I had just returned from the Gulf War, and that's what they wanted to hear about. They wanted to hear about the challenges of operating in the desert. What were the lessons learned? What went well and what areas needed improvement. The briefing was at the unclassified level, so there was only so much information that could disclose in such a setting. At times, the question and answer period would last longer than my presentation. The discussion would often extend into "happy hour" at the local officer's club. I was also asked to lecture on leadership to the young midshipmen at their Naval Academy in Rio de Janeiro. I found this experience extremely rewarding.

However, in retrospect the smart move would have been to turn down the assignment to Brazil, go to Headquarters Marine Corps and keep the family together. As one moves up the rank structure, it's imperative to have high-level staff duty. Duty at headquarters brings with it exposure to senior officers who one day may be sitting on your promotion board. I was selected to lieutenant colonel while in Brazil. For my service in Brazil, I was awarded the Brazilian "Medalha de Merrito Itamerreti." I had to obtain permission from Headquarters Marine Corps (HQMC) before accepting a foreign award. Permission from Headquarters Marine Corps was subsequently granted without any problem. My billet sponsor from HQMC accompanied me to the Brazilian embassy in Washington, DC, for the formal presentation. Overall, I thought I had a very rewarding professional tour.

Upon my return from Brazil, I was assigned to Quantico, Virginia, as per my request. However, upon reporting, I was told that I had been reassigned to a new unit that was being set up from scratch, called the Marine Air Ground Task Force Staff Training Program, or MSTP. The unit was put together to help marine corps units implement lessons learned from the country's experience in desert warfare from operations in Desert Shield and Desert Storm. I would be handling the command and control aspect of the course. I met many talented officers in that organization. Several would later be promoted to general officers. One became commandant of the Marine Corps. Shortly after I joined the MSTP, I was selected to command a marine squadron on the West Coast. While I was assigned to the MSTP, I had the opportunity to serve on a promotion board that was convened to cover the Marine Corps' two top enlisted ranks, E-8 and E-9. Since each of those pay grades included two ranks, we actually covered four promotion boards. It took us a total of nine weeks working ten-hour days. I was with the MSTP for only twenty months before I left to command the West Coast squadron. Upon my departure from the MSTP, I was awarded another Navy Commendation Medal. The truth is that I always felt a little like a fish out of water with the MSTP. There were a lot of smart officers there. They covered material with which the field commanders were familiar with and receptive to many of the ideas presented. However, command and control was new and not always well received. My pitch was basically that command and control is the art and the science of warfare. It is two sides of the same coin. A commander's decision is based on his experience, knowledge and wisdom. That constitutes the command aspect of warfare. One could say, that it's the art of warfare. Technology such as communications and radar are examples of the means by which a commander exercises control. This constitutes the science of warfare. Unfortunately, many of the senior commanders were not receptive to this new topic. They see this as someone trying to tell them how to do their job. My initial suggestion was to have the team leader introduce the topic, than turn it over to me. I was told my suggestion would be taken under consideration. Although the MSTP concept was a great success, the command and control part was less so.

I assumed command of the Marine Air Control Squadron in April 1995, the day after the Oklahoma City bombing. The Marine Air Control Group (MACG) had two identical Air Control Squadrons, and I was originally scheduled to take over our sister squadron in Yuma, Arizona. But Yuma was remote from the highly specialized medical care my daughter Carla needed on a regular basis. Therefore, during a trip to the West Coast the year prior, I approached the group commander about the possibility of switching to Camp Pendleton. The change of command was scheduled within a couple of months of each other, so I didn't see a problem. Once I finished briefing him on my family situation, his answer was emphatic "You need to go to Camp Pendleton". I informed the incoming group commander of my conversation with the current group commander. His response to my request was not pleasant. The incoming commander's reaction was not pleasant. He said "You can take care of any medical appointments when you came up to El Toro for our monthly commanders' conference." I left things there. Six months later, I received orders from Headquarters Marine Corps (HQMC) to report to Camp Pendleton California and assume command of Marine Air Control Squadron 1.

Apparently, the incoming commander never forgave me for what he considered my end around him. I didn't know him well, but I knew about his reputation. You didn't want to get on his bad side. I had no choice but to approach the previous group commander, because he was still in charge when I assumed command of the squadron.

Commanding a squadron or battalion of marines is the aspiration of every marine officer I have ever known. It is demanding in terms of time and can often be frustrating, but it is also extremely satisfying and rewarding. I had the honor and privilege of leading this squadron of outstanding marines for two years. They were the best two years by far of my thirty-year Marine Corps career.

However, there were things going on that indirectly affected me. The new group commander had a drinking problem. After the military police caught him drinking a twelve-pack for lunch in the parking lot of the base gas station, he spent six weeks in alcohol rehabilitation. It was all very hush-hush, but it was hard to keep the information from the unit commanders with whom he dealt on a daily basis. The evaluations of every one of his subordinate commanders would be indirectly affected because his reputation was diminished. The importance of his opinion of our performance also was diminished. When I received my yearly performance evaluation from him, I was a bit disappointed. I was not disappointed by what was in the report—it was flattering enough, and I was ranked first of the eight unit commanders in the group—but my earlier experience on a promotion board revealed that there were two key elements missing. I was not recommended for promotion or for top-level school. The marine corps promotes roughly 50 percent of its first-time-eligible lieutenant colonels to full colonel. Having been selected for, and having completed a successful command tour put me in a pretty good position. I was awarded the Meritorious Service Medal, an award presented by the president of the United States, although it is often delegated to subordinate commanders of three stars or above. A copy of the citation appears as appendix 2. The list for promotion to colonel came out in the spring of 1997, and my name wasn't on it. I was disappointed but not completely surprised. I don't want to rationalize, but if it looks like a duck, walks like a duck, and swims like a duck, chances are it's not a chicken. It could have been a coincidence, but sometimes things were just what they looked like. I had gotten on the commander's bad side, and I had paid the price.

Mario V. Carmo

Commanding a squadron of marines took a lot of my time, but I tried to spend as much time as possible with my daughters Patricia and Carla on weekends. I would often take Patricia out for a run with me. At first she struggled, but soon she picked up a few techniques that made running easier for her. She developed a love for running and ran several marathons, including the Marine Corps marathon after she graduated from college.

The local school district didn't have enough classrooms for the number of students enrolled, so it devised a plan for year-round school. Kids would attend classes for three months and then have a month off. This went on continuously—hence the term "year-round school." Patricia went to school there during the fifth, sixth, and seventh grades. She received a small weekly allowance that was tied to some tasks she had to perform. In fifth grade, she was looking for a way to increase her allowance, so I got her started on reading Nancy Drew books. She got an extra dollar for every book she read. She had to tell me about each book and answer a couple of questions about the plot, which was my way of ensuring she had read and understood the book. She devoured these books. We would go to the local library every Saturday morning and pick up three or four. Soon, we were having a hard time finding books from the series she hadn't read.

The country was going through the Beanie Babies craze around 1995–96. Patricia was spending all of her allowance on the toys, and she was looking for a way to increase her allowance. Since she was reading so much and so well, I figured the next step was to start her on writing book reports. We renegotiated her allowance to five dollars per book report. The first one was difficult. She kept saying, "Why can't I just tell you about it?" That was not our deal. I worked with her on developing the opening paragraph. It had to contain at least three complete sentences. Next, we worked on the main theme of the book. Finally, we would write up a summary. The way I explained it to her was the way we had learned the techniques of military instruction in the marines: tell them what you are going to tell them, tell them, and then tell them what you told them. Our deal was that she would keep rewriting the book reports until I was satisfied. This led to a few cases of "this is unfair," but she kept plugging away. Once she got the hang of it, she wrote twenty-one book reports between the months of June and January in sixth grade. She developed an excellent command of the English language. She offered to edit this manuscript, but I declined. I'm sure she would have done an excellent job.

When my two years of commanding the squadron came to an end, as all good things do, I had the option of moving out of Southern California or staying in the area for another year. As the Marine Air Control Group (MACG) executive officer. In layman's terms, I would be the second-in-command of eight battalion-size units consisting of 3,500 marines. The group headquarters was in El Toro, California, approximately sixty-five miles north of my residence. Yet, I decided to stay because this option gave my family more stability. I was able to keep my elder daughter in a familiar environment. Other than the drive, my year as the group executive officer was uneventful. My boss was a great guy to work for. Other than our routine training, our biggest project was getting the base ready to turn over to Orange County. The days of not one, but two Marine Corps bases within ten miles of each other in the densely populated Orange County, California, had come to an end. The real estate was just too valuable. After much complaining from the local population, Congress decided to close the helicopter base in Tustin and the fixed wing base in El Toro, and move marine aviation south the Camp Pendleton and Miramar, just north of San Diego.

The list for colonel came out in the spring of 1998, and again my name wasn't on it. An officer's best chance for promotion was always the first time he was eligible. Every year, there would often be a few name from what the Marine Corps called "above zone", but one's chances were very low. After the second year, an officer's chances of promotion are extremely rare.

In the summer of 1997, I decided to take the whole family on a vacation to Portugal. This would give the girls an opportunity to get to know their grandparents and vice versa. I had the opportunity to show the girls around my hometown of Chaves in addition to showing them the sanctuary in Braga and some of the historical monuments in Lisbon.

When it came time to leave Southern California in the summer of 1998, Headquarters Marine Corps gave me two options. I could either fill the billet of war plans officer at the US European Command in Stuttgart, Germany, or go to the Naval Space Command in Dahlgren, Virginia, as the deputy director for operation and intelligence. Both jobs required a top-secret clearance which I had. I chose the latter.

During this time, it became evident to both me and my wife that our marriage was in trouble. All the commuting and the long hours at work had left very little time for me to help raise our children. I tried to be engaged with Patricia on weekends, but Carla was another matter altogether. She needed constant attention, and my wife had taken on most of the burden.

I realized my career was essentially over, but I wasn't ready to retire. I didn't know what I wanted to do after all these years in uniform. I didn't know how much longer I would remain on active duty, but I wasn't ready to leave yet. I had a two-year obligation if I accepted these orders. My wife and I decided that she would go back to our home in Connecticut with the two girls, while I went off to my next assignment in Virginia alone. I tried to make the seven-hundred-mile round trip every two to three weeks, but it wasn't always possible due to the requirements of my job. The distance and my absence exacerbated our marriage situation. Meanwhile, Patricia was going through adolescence. I have always heard that you can always tell an adolescent, but you can't tell them much. On the weekends I was at home, things weren't much better. It is difficult for a parent to impose house rules when he is away most of the time.

This is a common problem for military families. This situation placed additional pressure on our marriage.

Two years into my tour at Naval Space Command, the officer monitor at HQMC agreed to move me back to Quantico, Virginia. The move would include taking my wife and daughters from Connecticut to Quantico. My wife declined the move, and I decided to stay at Space Command. My job there was exhausting. I was on duty practically 24/7. I had a special phone installed in my living quarters called a STU III, and it was encrypted up to "Secret". Conversations seldom got beyond "Sir, you need to come in".

Part of my job was to supervise a group of scientists who maintained a catalog of all the debris in space—or at least all the debris we had the capability of tracking, which was anything bigger than seventy centimeters. We tracked primarily large rocket engines that had peeled off in lower orbits. Many of these ended up reentering the atmosphere and burning up upon reentry. However, based on the angle of entry, some would break up into smaller pieces upon reentry. When they broke up, our mission was to locate and number the pieces. We also had to identify their new orbits. Once that was done, we ensured the pieces were entered in the space catalog. Sometimes we could locate a dozen pieces in a couple of days. At other times, it would take our scientists weeks to locate a single piece. Debris flying around space without a known orbit is a hazard to our many communications and imagery satellites. A one-centimeter piece of debris flying at seventeen thousand miles per hour can take out a hundred-million-dollar satellite. Despite our knowing the locations of space debris and trying to maneuver around many known items in space, both active and inactive, there is an element of risk in all space operations. Once a satellite is established on an orbit, it is maneuvered out of that orbit only in very extreme cases. One of these is for national operational requirements. A second would be a possible collision with another satellite or debris. These decisions are made at the highest level of the command, with both military and scientific recommendations. The launching of a satellite is analogous to buying a car with a tank full of gasoline, but once you use all the gas, you can no longer move the car. Satellites are launched with a limited amount of fuel because of weight considerations. Once the fuel is expended, you no longer have the flexibility to move the satellite out of its orbit.

In 1981, my parents retired and moved back to Portugal. At this point, they had spent seventeen years in the United States. Their children were settled with the exception of my youngest bother Rui who had just graduated from high school. They had achieved what they had set out to do, bring their children to a country where opportunities were available to those who were willing to work for them. My dad was sixty-two, my mother was fifty five, but they were both physically and psychologically exhausted and had aged beyond their years. My dad had not worked a single day during the recession of 1974-1975. He was also unemployed during the recession of 1979-1981. The unemployment rate at the time was around nine percent. No company wants a sixty-year old laborer who had a difficult time with the English language, if they could get someone half his age with whom you could communicate. There was a lot to pick from. Furthermore, my dad did not drive. He became more and more discouraged. My mother's health condition exacerbated the situation and finally tipped the scales. She had suffered from angina, which is a form of coronary heart disease for years, but had continued to work. After the second acute attacks at work where the ambulance had to be called, the company let her go. They were concerned about liability if she passed away in their premises after a couple of clear cut warnings. My mother didn't know enough to go to the Social Security Office and apply for disability. Without any source of income, and few prospects of my dad finding a job, it made their decision to return to Portugal a sensible one. My mother was only fifty-five and did not yet qualify for Social Security, but my dad was sixty-two and qualified for reduced Social security retirement. He also had a small pension from his ten years of work as a member of the local

Laborers' union. They purchased a three bedroom apartment when they arrived. They were very frugal. They were able to live on my father's very modest pension.

They had been living there alone for twenty years, with the exception of an occasional summer visit from me or one of my siblings. They were now getting on in years. They often complained that they raised six children and were living their golden years alone. They encouraged me to retire and return to Portugal. In light of everything going on in my personal life, I decided that this might not be a bad idea.

My last year at Naval Space Command had been extremely difficult. I was burned out. It was a combination of the demands of the job and what was going on in my personal life. I talked to my boss, and he brought up the issue with the admiral. It was agreed that I would take over as the N-5 plans officer, focusing primarily on Marine Corps requirements. However, shortly after taking over, I suffered an accident. During one of my weekend visits to Connecticut, I fell off a ladder while painting our home. I came down headfirst and tried to break the fall with my right hand. I ended up breaking many of the small bones in my right wrist. After several surgeries and months of physical therapy, the hand surgeon decided to fuse the wrist. The pain should have stopped, but it never did. It hurts to this day.

I retired on October 1, 2002. During my retirement ceremony, I was awarded my second Meritorious Service Medal. Again, it was awarded by the president of the United States (George W. Bush) but signed by the chief of naval operations, Admiral Clark. The citation appears as appendix 3. Shortly after I retired, I packed a few things and moved to Portugal.

I remember a conversation I had with my daughter Patricia just prior to my departure. She was a junior in high school. During my absence, she had gotten a little lazy, and her grades reflected the obvious lack of effort. One weekend while I was home, we had a long discussion about the importance of a formal education. I made it clear that it wasn't a question of *if* but rather *where* she would be attending college. It was then that I relayed to her a saying that I had heard in a John Wayne movie many years ago. I believe the movie was *Sands of Iwo Jima*, made in the 1950s. John Wayne played a marine sergeant counseling a young marine in a way that only marine sergeants can. He put his arm around the shoulder of the young marine and said, "You know, son, life is hard, but it's harder if you are stupid." Patricia got the message. That saying became sort of a joke between us. A few years ago, she gave me a plaque with that saying. I proudly hung it in my office and have included it in this book. Early in her senior year, she decided she wanted to be a guidance counselor. We discussed the requirement for a master's degree. She was fine with six years of post–high school education. I suggested that she might want to go into teaching and later make a lateral move into counseling, but she was committed to being a guidance counselor. Her passion and desire must have shown through because she was hired straight out of her internship. She is still passionate about her job twelve years later. Not many people have the luxury of working in a profession they love. She has married and has two wonderful children; Walker who is two and half and Lia who is four months old. I'm so proud of the person she has become.

The divorce was final in May 2003, one week before Patricia's high school graduation. I returned from Portugal for her graduation. Patricia stayed behind in Connecticut with an aunt to attend junior college, and I returned to take care of my parents. Later that fall, I returned to Connecticut to provide Patricia with a little more guidance and support. I stayed in Connecticut until late spring of 2004. Patricia ended the school year and returned to Florida to rejoin her mother. Once Patricia left, there was no need for me to remain in Connecticut and I returned to Portugal.

CHAPTER 7

ADJUSTING TO RETIRED LIFE

When I arrived in Portugal, I was not sure I would be able to adapt. I had left when I was twelve years old. Sure, I had been back many times on vacation to see my parents, friends, and relatives, but living there permanently was different. I rented an apartment near my parents' home and bought a car. Early on, I had lunch with my parents daily and made a point of compensating my mother for the expenses as was my obligation. Neither of my parents drove a car, so I was glad to be able to take them to doctor's appointments and on short trips here and there. We would go out to lunch every Sunday at my dad's favorite restaurant. With time, it became my favorite as well. I developed a great relationship with the owner. A group of us would go hunting during hunting season. There was not much game, but we made a day of great camaraderie out of it. My parents loved octopus, and there was no place where they made it like in the province of Galiza in Spain. The three of us would go three times per month, like clockwork. Two years after I arrived in Portugal, I decided to buy a single-family home and upgraded my car. I was adapting to everyday life without much difficulty. I decided to stay and take care of my parents for as long as was necessary.

I discovered an international organization called Rotary. I had heard of it in the US but didn't know there was a club in Chaves. The club's major community project was a university for seniors. I was asked to teach English. After five years, I was asked to join the Rotary Club. That ended up occupying more and more of my time. After a few years, I took over as club president. The city of Chaves had ceded the club an old elementary school, which we converted to meet our special needs.

In the spring of 2007, I discovered a tumor in my neck while shaving. That same day, I went to see my primary care physician. He took one look, felt around it, and called a colleague at the emergency room of the local hospital. I was admitted and administered the standard blood tests. The results came back normal, so a needle biopsy was performed. My attending physician called me aside and said, "I'm not going to sugarcoat it—we find what we find. You have cancer. The biopsy came back positive for lymphoma."

I was discharged the following morning and made plans to fly to San Diego, California. My sister lived there, and I still had some contacts there from my days on active duty. I had connections at the naval hospital because of my previous hand surgery. After another biopsy, it was determined that the cancer was follicular lymphoma.

Patricia was graduating from college at Florida State in a couple of weeks, so the doctor and I decided to hold off treatment until after my trip to Tallahassee for the ceremony. Once I returned, we implemented the cancer treatment plan recommended by my attending oncologist. I underwent chemotherapy, which consisted of a cocktail of drugs once every three weeks. Each treatment took the better part of a day. Using a pickup truck borrowed from my sister's neighbor Roger, I drove myself to and from the hospital because my sister and brother-in-law were both working at the time. The drive back after treatment was difficult, but I managed to do it. During the first week of the treatment, I felt terrible. I didn't want to see or speak with anyone. The second week was a little better. By the third week, I started to feel almost normal. The following week, I started the cycle all over again. My cancer treatment program consisted of six cycles, or eighteen weeks. Once the treatment was completed, a PET scan indicated that my tumor had been reduced by two-thirds. It was a good result according to the oncologist. He also told me I would be a good candidate for the Rituximab maintenance program. The maintenance program was four weekly treatments every six months for two years. Rituximab was the first synthetic approved drug for cancer treatment at the time. It was very expensive. I was told it went for twenty thousand dollars a dose on the open market. Once treatment was over, I returned to Portugal.

When I returned to San Diego six months later, my oncologist had some bad news for me. The PET scan showed that the tumor had grown back to near its original size. After much discussion, we decided that the best course of action was to stay with the Rituximab maintenance program but add thirty treatments of radiation. The radiation completely burned the tumor. Unfortunately, it also burned the top half of my left lung, in addition to several teeth from my left lower jaw. I continued with the Rituximab maintenance program for two years, as originally planned. I traveled between Portugal and San Diego, California, every six months. In August 2010, I was declared cancer-free.

Back in Portugal, my parents' health started to fail shortly after my initial cancer diagnosis. My father was in his late eighties at the time, and my mother was five years younger. Until the summer of 2008, when my father suffered a cerebral hemorrhage, they both had been incredibly healthy for people their age. My father's condition was serious. He was evacuated from the local hospital in Chaves to the hospital of Santo Antonio in Porto. After a couple of weeks in Porto, where the local surgeons drilled several holes in his skull to relieve the pressure, he was returned to Chaves. Once he was in Chaves, the hospital said there was nothing else they could do, and he could recover at home. My father had never had a high threshold for pain. He complained about everything. My mother simply couldn't take care of him. I set out looking for a placement in a nursing home. My dad did not want to go. My mother had long ago promised to join him in the nursing home if either of them had to be committed. Now she was having second thoughts.

I hired several local women to keep my mother company and help her with light housework, but they never lasted long. My mother was difficult to get along with. She had a very strong personality and liked being in control. Her efforts to control my siblings and me, even as adults, had led to some hard feelings at times. My dad was more passive. He didn't mind letting her handle things, from finances to discipline of the children. It was an arrangement that seemed to work for them. They were married for sixty-six years.

Through my contacts in Rotary, I managed to get my father placed in a home and to get a couples' room. It was part of a national chain, but this particular home had only fifteen patients. Again, my mother was reluctant to join my dad, but after six months of being alone in the apartment, she finally agreed to join him. I was lucky the home kept that bed available for six months. It was made clear to me that compensation was expected, and I complied willingly. I visited my parents daily and took them out to lunch on Sundays.

In January 2009, just a few days before I was to travel to San Diego for my semiannual treatment, I received terrible news. My oldest sister called to inform me that my younger sister, Micky, had passed away. She was just fifty-five, but she had lived a life of torment. Her marriage had been complicated from the beginning. Her home's water and electricity had been turned off on numerous occasions. She had fought anorexia, bulimia, depression, and alcohol abuse. Her divorce a couple of years earlier had left her holding the short end of the stick. She had three children. Only the oldest was married; the other two were still in school. The circumstances of her death were unclear but not a total surprise. I changed my flight for the next day and attended the funeral services in Connecticut on my way to my scheduled treatment in San Diego.

Micky had been my father's favorite. He had always imagined that she would be the one taking care of him in his old age. My mother and I decided not to tell him of her passing. We wanted to spare him the pain. My dad's health was never the same after his cerebral hemorrhage. He had periodic mini strokes from which he would recover partially, but never completely. The effects of these mini strokes became cumulative. During one of his visits to the local hospital, he caught pneumonia. A couple of days later, in November 2009, he passed away. He was ninety years old.

My mother continued to live in the nursing home, but she became increasingly more difficult to deal with. She would often complain that there were items missing from her room. I believe this was largely as a result of her advanced years. They ranged from money to sweaters and other pieces of clothing. Of course, she would make sure all the employees knew about her missing items. In Portugal, individuals who work in elder care facilities are mostly poor women. They may not have much in terms of material means, but they had their honor and dignity. Accusing someone either directly or indirectly of stealing, is a great insult. On many occasions, one of them would get my attention as I walked in the building and make me aware that my mother was once again, very upset because of something was missing from her room. I would take a look around with my mother and would always find whatever she was missing. Sometime it was an item she and I, had returned to my parents' home because of the lack of space at the home. Meanwhile, the damage had been done. I would have another clean up on isle four. I would go around and apologize to the employees. This normally consisted of a small token.

A reasonable time after my father passed away, the home moved another patient in with my mother as I expected. I had worked with the home during this transition period and tried to prepare my mother for this eventuality. She was reluctant to have anyone come in and "take my father's place". However, I tried to make her see that there was a long list of people waiting for admission to the home. She went through several roommates before we settled on one she could get along with. Her new roommate had suffered a stroke and was unable to speak. My mother couldn't provoke an argument if she wanted too. I continued to visit her on a daily basis, normally in the mornings before lunch. I also took her to doctor's appointments and kept our Sunday lunch routine at her favorite restaurant. When she was up to it, I would also take her to eat octopus in nearby Spain. However, nothing I did was ever enough. On one occasion, she was standing with her back to me in the corridor while complaining to the staff about something or other I had done or failed to do. Somewhere in the exchange, she referred to me as "that son of a bitch." One of the employees looked in my direction and cringed. I quietly turned and walked out.

CHAPTER 8

COMING HOME

In the spring of 2010, after my semiannual treatment in San Diego, I flew to Florida to see my daughter Patricia and decided to buy a home there. Patricia had obtained her master's degree in counseling psychology and was now working full-time as a guidance counselor in the local school system. She needed a place to live, and I also needed a base of operations from which to work during my visits to see her and her sister Carla. Buying our own place made sense. The real estate market had been in a freefall for a couple of years, so this was a good time to buy. Patricia lived in the home while I lived in Portugal for the majority of the year. During my visit to Florida the following year, I joined the local Portuguese American Cultural Center in Palm Coast. It was a great place to go and meet friends with similar interests. One of those interests was soccer, of course. At this time, my sister Linda and my brother-in-law Tony also decided to move from San Diego to Florida and settled in Palm Coast.

In Portugal, in addition to my Rotary Club friends and my hunting buddies, I also developed friendships with a group of about thirty-five that traveled throughout Europe every summer. The parish priest led the group, and we traveled to Italy, Spain, Germany, Austria, and all the Scandinavia countries, to name just a few. We developed close bonds and looked forward to these trips every summer.

In the spring of 2011, shortly after returning from one of my semiannual trips to Florida, I received a phone call from the US embassy in Lisbon. Apparently, someone at the Portuguese embassy was trying to contact me. After gathering some more information, I arrived at a conclusion and agreed to let the caller pass on my e-mail address. The daughter of a girl I had known in high school was trying to find her father. I'd had a brief romantic episode with the girl's mother just before I left for Vietnam. Once I was discharged from active duty in the spring of 1972, the issue of the paternity had been adjudicated in the local court. I took a blood test which was inconclusive. Medical technology in those days could exclude you, but not definitively determine positive paternity. After listening to both sides, the judge ruled that based on the preponderance of the evidence, it was more likely than not, that I was **not** the child's father. That was the end of the subject until apparently now. She reached out to me, and we had several pleasant exchanges by email. I later received her, and her husband, along with their three children in my house in Florida. We stay in touch but are not close. We see the world from diametrically opposing political viewpoints. In this day and age, this can and often is a source of friction.

Cancer has left me particularly sensitive to my body. I caught the tumor early on, and that is probably the reason I am still alive. I began having sharp pain in my left clavicle. It didn't seem natural. After months of discomfort, I decided to visit my oncologist during my trip to Florida in January 2013. She was dismissive of the pain, so I decided to seek a second opinion and another oncologist. With the help of a physician at the Naval Hospital in Jacksonville, I was able to schedule an appointment with an orthopedic oncologist at the Mayo Clinic in Jacksonville, Florida. She subsequently performed a bone biopsy and unfortunately confirmed my suspicion. It was cancer. The lymphoma had metastasized to my left clavicle. The recommended course of action surprisingly, was not additional chemo, but rather radiation treatments. After thirty treatments, the cancer cells had once again been eradicated. I have been cancer-free to this day, over nine years later. Knock on wood!

In June 2013, just three days before I was scheduled to return to Portugal, my mother passed away. The prolonged cancer treatment had forced me to postpone my return flight on three previous occasions. It appeared to have been pretty much what happened to my dad. She had endured several mini strokes, which had become more frequent with time. In the end, she succumbed to pneumonia. I was informed of her passing on a Friday night, but I was unable to get plane reservations until Sunday afternoon. A friend met me at the airport in Porto and we arrived in Chaves, hundred miles away, by 10:00 a.m. on Monday. I made all the arrangements with the funeral home over the phone before I departed Florida. The funeral home met me with the body at our village church in Faioes at 2:00 p.m. that same day. I sat with the body, received friends and family, essentially had the wake from two to five in the afternoon. At five, we had the funeral mass, followed by the burial at the local cemetery. She is buried in the same grave as my dad, her older brother Antonio, and his wife Carolina.

With both of my parents deceased, I no longer felt a need or a desire to remain in Portugal. My daughters needed me much more in Florida. I placed my home on the market and sold it in two weeks. This was unheard of. It was a bad time economically for the country. I saw houses which had been on the market for ten years in Chaves. I sold my house to a couple who had lived in the United States and were returning to Portugal after losing their only son in a firearms accident. After spending thirty years dealing with Marines on active duty, you learn to read people. They were nice folks so, I took a chance. I actually accepted a personal check as payment for the house. We closed the deal in two weeks.

I also decided to take on the burden of liquidating my parents' estate. I paid all my siblings fair market value for their shares. Eight years later, I'm still trying to sell some of the assets. The hard part hasn't been so much the value of the estate, but the burden of dealing with siblings, relatives and the Portuguese bureaucracy.

The first thing I did upon moving back to Florida for good in 2013, was join one of the three local Rotary Clubs. The area has one club that meets for breakfast, one for lunch, and a third for dinner. I joined the Rotary Club of Flagler Beach, which meets for breakfast in the hall of my church on Thursday mornings. I tried living in Portugal during the summer months to avoid the Florida humidity but found it just as hot and humid during the last several years. Although I continue to visit Portugal on an annual basis, my visits have gotten much shorter.

In 2015, I decided to take on a personal challenge. I put together a team to run the local Portuguese American Cultural Center (PACC) for a year. As president, I essentially accepted a full time job without a salary. With every successive year, it becomes a bigger and bigger challenge to find enough volunteers to run the day to day operations of the Club. I wasn't quite sure what I was getting into, but with the encouragement and the offer to help of a couple of veterans, I decided to take on the job. I had no illusions. I knew the job would bring little praise and much criticism. We managed to add a couple of offices to expand our administrative space by renovating one of the bathrooms. We also managed to double the size of our parking capacity. The PACC is an organization of approximately one thousand members. A good portion, perhaps 30 percent, is seasonal residents of Florida. The organization is run primarily by volunteers. Members volunteer based on the relationships they have with board members. I was new to the community and knew very few of the members. Despite many challenges, we managed to keep the team together and have a highly successful year.

I dated on and off while in Palm Coast and used online services like most people my age. In the twenty-first century, this seems to be the way to go. Most encounters were a disappointment, primarily because people often misrepresent who they are. People post clean-cut twenty-year-old pictures then, show up with arms full of tattoos. They post that they have professional degrees but cannot put two sentences together. They are clearly inarticulate. They claim to be financially independent but, are working part-time jobs to help ends meet. I had practically given up meeting anyone of quality, when I met a wonderful woman named Wanda. She intrigued me from the very first date. I had a feeling that I was dealing with a quality person. After dating for a year and half, we decided to move in together. A year later, we were married. We complement each other so well, that I can honestly say that I am incomplete without her. She has turned out to be the soul mate we all search for but seldom find. I consider myself extremely lucky to have found her. We live in a great home in a gated community, with a wonderful view of an island green on a golf course. We are both financially secure and love to travel. We have been to Scotland, Ireland, China, Egypt, Spain and Portugal together. We have several other trips planned. I am looking forward to a wonderful life together.

Because of my many ailments derived from thirty years on active duty, the Veterans Administration declared me totally and permanently disabled. My health is not great, but considering the abuse my body has taken from thirty years of active duty, it could be worst. In the Marine Corps, we use to say that years in the Corps are like dog years. Now I see why. Cumulative they take quiet a toll on your body.

In 2019, my daughter Patricia married Austin Weeks. Nine months later, she gave birth to their first child. They named him Walker. Two years later she gave birth to a baby girl named Lia. I have a wonderful relationship with her. Despite her busy schedule, we try to see each other at least once per week. My younger brothers live in Connecticut. We all try to stay in touch, but relationships have to be nurtured. We don't see each other nearly as much as we all know we should. The experiences of our early years were identical, but as adults, we have gone in different directions. Consequently, we have become very different people. My oldest sister and I have lived in the same city for the last seven years but have just casual contact. I will be eternally grateful for the help she gave me while I went through chemotherapy in San Diego where she lived. Life has not always been easy, but I have always faced it the only way I know: head-on and with hard work and perseverance. I have tried to make the best of the cards I was dealt. I try to live by that old saying: "There's no sense in complaining. Eighty percent of the people don't care, and the other twenty percent are glad you are having problems." As I write this manuscript, we have been under various types of restrictions over the last two years due to a nationally declared pandemic caused by COVID-19. We are fully vaccinated and have been very lucky to have been spared from the virus. We have not been as fortunate with our travel plans. We have had several planned cruise trips canceled. However, this too shall pass! We hope!

The Secretary of the Navy takes pleasure in presenting the
NAVY COMMENDATION MEDAL to

MAJOR MARIO V. CARMO

UNITED STATES MARINE CORPS

for service as set forth in the following
CITATION:

"For meritorious achievement in the superior performance of
his duties while serving as the day watch Tactical Air Control
Center, Tactical Aviation Coordinator for Marine Central Command,
and Marine Liaison to United States Central Command Air Force,
Saudi Arabia, from 24 August 1990 to 8 March 1991. During this
period, Major Carmo served as the principal point of contact on
day watch between the United States Air Force Tactical Air
Control Center and the Marine Corps Tactical Air Control Center
for aviation matters. As the senior watch officer, he was the
architect of the Marine Central Command approach to integration
of Marine aviation into joint and combined combat operations.
Major Carmo provided critical Joint Forces Aircraft Control
Center aviation support for engaged Marine Central Command forces
during the ground campaign. Through his personal dedication and
attention to duty, the Computer Force Management System was kept
updated with the best available information on the flow of Marine
Central Command aviation sorties. In addition, he ensured that
critical Marine Central Command fire support coordination
measures were distributed promptly and accurately. Major Carmo's
motivation, initiative, and dedication to duty throughout,
reflected great credit upon himself, and upheld the highest
traditions of the Marine Corps, and the United States Naval
Service."

For the Secretary of the Navy,

W. E. BOOMER
Lieutenant General, U. S. Marine Corps
Commanding General, I Marine Expeditionary Force

Citation for a Navy Commendation Medal awarded for my
tour during operation Desert Shield/ Desert Storm 1991

The President of the United States takes pleasure in presenting the
MERITORIOUS SERVICE MEDAL to

LIEUTENANT COLONEL MARIO V. CARMO

UNITED STATES MARINE CORPS

for service as set forth in the following

CITATION:

For outstanding meritorious service while serving as Commanding
Officer, Marine Air Control Squadron 1, Marine Air Control Group 38, 3d
Marine Aircraft Wing, U.S. Marine Forces, Pacific from April 1995 to April
1997. Throughout this period, Lieutenant Colonel Carmo performed his
duties in an exemplary and highly professional manner. Through his
exceptional leadership, the squadron contributed significantly to the testing
and development of the Theater Missile Defense system. Under Lieutenant
Colonel Carmo's command, the unit provided superb Marine Air Command
and Control System support during many major training exercises.
Lieutenant Colonel Carmo demonstrated outstanding ability to conceive and
guide programs that improved logistics, supply, maintenance, training, and
administration in the squadron resulting in a superb state of readiness.
Lieutenant Colonel Carmo's untiring efforts to carry out his demanding tasks
with unfailing good judgment, effectiveness, and total devotion to duty were
in keeping with the highest traditions of the Marine Corps and the United
States Naval Service.

For the President,

JEFFERSON D. HOWELL, JR.
LIEUTENANT GENERAL, U.S. MARINE CORPS
COMMANDER, U.S. MARINE FORCES, PACIFIC

Citation for a Meritorious Service Medal awarded for my tour of
duty as Commanding Office, Marine Air Control Squadron 1

Chief of Naval Operations

The President of the United States takes pleasure in presenting the
MERITORIOUS SERVICE MEDAL (Gold Star in lieu of the Second Award) to

LIEUTENANT COLONEL MARIO V. CARMO
UNITED STATES MARINE CORPS

for service as set forth in the following

CITATION:

For outstanding meritorious service as Deputy Director
Operations and Intelligence Division, Naval Space Command, Dahlgren,
Virginia from July 1998 to July 2002. Throughout his tour,
Lieutenant Colonel Carmo demonstrated exemplary performance and
leadership. In directing the execution of operations for a division
of approximately 100 military and 50 civilian personnel, he was
instrumental to the provision of non-stop space support to worldwide
naval forces, U.S. Space Command, and over 800 national and
Department of Defense activities. As Deputy for Intelligence and
Operations, he executed the implementation of several major
revisions in the provision of space support, notably, the overhaul
of the Command's operational watch structure to improve round-the-
clock Fleet and Marine Force responsiveness and the initiation of
Naval Space Command's role in Counterspace Operations. Additionally,
he led the establishment of Naval Space as the System Operational
Manager for military and commercial satellite communications used by
all Naval and Joint forces, implementation of global and regional
satellite communication support centers for integrated worldwide
support, and the overhaul of major command systems in preparation
for the year 2000 and other crucial rollover dates. His superb
handling of the myriad of complex and wide reaching technical issues
and decisions to manage the daily operations and intelligence
missions at Naval Space Command was a key cornerstone of our command
success. Lieutenant Colonel Carmo's many outstanding accomplishments
contributed immeasurably to achieving national military objectives
and advancing joint, as well as Naval, Space capabilities and
readiness. Lieutenant Colonel Carmo's professionalism, achievements
and loyal devotion to duty reflected great credit upon him and were
in keeping with the highest traditions of the Marine Corps and the
United States Naval Service.

For the President,

V. E. CLARK
Admiral, United States Navy
Chief of Naval Operations

Citation from My second Merritorious Service
Medal from Naval Space Command

Printed in the United States
by Baker & Taylor Publisher Services